Reclaiming Our Priestly Character

Father David L. Toups

THE INSTITUTE FOR PRIESTLY FORMATION
IPF PUBLICATIONS

Endorsements

"In *Reclaiming Our Priestly Character*, Father David Toups links a careful theological study of priesthood with a wise and practical spirituality. This rare and much needed synthesis will greatly benefit priests, seminarians, indeed, anyone in the Church who cares about the renewal of the priesthood."

- Fr. Louis J. Cameli, S.T.D.

"*Reclaiming Our Priestly Character* offers a review of the present crisis and shows the way forward to a renovation of the priesthood that is in keeping with both the perennial wisdom of the Catholic tradition and the teaching of the Second Vatican Council."

- George Weigel

"The Biblical and historical foundations articulated in this artful book make it a 'must read' for anyone desiring to receive a foundational understanding of the Sacrament of Holy Orders in the living tradition of the Church."

- Dr. Scott Hahn

The Institute for Priestly Formation
Mission Statement

The Institute for Priestly Formation was founded to assist bishops in the spiritual formation of diocesan seminarians and priests in the Roman Catholic Church. The Institute responds to the need to foster spiritual formation as the integrating and governing principle of all aspects of priestly formation. Inspired by the biblical-evangelical spirituality of Ignatius Loyola, this spiritual formation has as its goal the cultivation of a deep interior communion with Christ; from such communion the priest shares in Christ's own pastoral charity. In carrying out its mission, the Institute directly serves diocesan seminarians and priests as well as those who are responsible for diocesan priestly formation.

THE INSTITUTE FOR PRIESTLY FORMATION
Creighton University
2500 California Plaza
Omaha, Nebraska 68178
www.creighton.edu/ipf
ipf@creighton.edu

NIHIL OBSTAT: Ed Hogan, Ph.D.

IMPRIMATUR: † Most Reverend Robert J. Carlson
                                    Bishop of Saginaw

THE INSTITUTE FOR PRIESTLY FORMATION
IPF PUBLICATIONS
2500 California Plaza
Omaha, Nebraska 68178
www.IPFpublications.com

Printed in the United States of America
ISBN -13: 978-0-9800455-0-5
ISBN-10: 0-9800455-0-9

Cover design by Timothy D. Boatright
Marketing Associates, U.S.A.
Tampa, Florida

Dedication

To my Dad, who taught me how to be a father.

Leon H. Toups

September 28, 1938 - September 5, 2006

Table of Contents

Chapter 3

The Foundation of the Priestly Life:

Preface

Being a child of God and serving Him is a joy to those who faithfully and lovingly live their vocation. This is true for all Christians, but for the priest, the ramifications of not doing so are catastrophic. As Blessed Columba Marmion wrote, "There could be no more fatal error for the priest than to underestimate the sacerdotal dignity. He must, on the contrary, have a very high conception of it."[1]

In a day and age in which permanent commitments are devalued by our society and in a particular way the priesthood is under attack for the sins of a small percentage, it is of utmost importance to re-emphasize both the permanence and the dignity of the calling to the ministerial priesthood. Even beyond these, the presbyterate seems divided along generational lines. The intention of *Reclaiming our Priestly Character* is to serve as a source of renewal for the priesthood.

Studies show that priests who have a solid understanding of the sacramental character received at ordination are more likely to be content and faithful in their vocation than those who do not. Pope John Paul II noted, "Knowledge of the nature and mission of the ministerial priesthood is an essential presupposition [...]" (*PDV* 11).

The priest must know who he is in order that he might act and serve in a manner appropriate to his state in life: *agere sequitur esse* – "doing follows being."[2] An integration of priestly identity and the call to love and serve is the call of today's priests. Now is the time for us to reclaim the gift received at ordination and joyfully serve the Bride of Christ so as to witness to the beauty of our vocation.

We need not be afraid or ashamed of being priests in the world today. The Lord and His Church need us to be who we are. By renewing our understanding of the priestly character, we are not saying that we are better than the lay faithful (and certainly not guaranteeing that we are holier), but that we *are* different by virtue of ordination (cf. *Lumen Gentium* 10). The more a priest recognizes the "gift received through the laying on of hands" (2 Timothy 1:6) the more he can allow the priestly character to animate the whole of his life of love and service to the people of God; this character is a dynamism for pastoral charity and holiness. We do the Church and ourselves a disservice when we deny the ontological reality of who we are – either theologically or functionally. Let us glorify God and edify (literally build-up) the Body of Christ by living with great enthusiasm the ministerial priesthood of Jesus Christ the great High Priest.

The root of this work is my doctoral dissertation completed at the *Angelicum* in Rome, which explains the plentiful endnotes following each chapter. I have purposefully left many references in for two reasons: the first is for the reading enthusiast who wants to go deeper; and the second, is as a reminder that this work is not simply my own opinion or perspective.

I am grateful to my thesis director, Fr. Robert Christian, O.P., and for the guidance and direction I have received from two deacons who have helped to make this current edition come to the light of day: Deacon Ronald Rojas, Ph.D. and Deacon James Keating, Ph.D. I would also like to acknowledge Jessi Kary, A.O., from the Pro Sanctity Movement, for her attentive editing. In order to frame this book within the context of integrated spirituality taught at the Institute for Priestly Formation, I have asked Fr. Jim Rafferty, who has been actively involved with the Institute for a number of years, to write the *Prologue*. *Reclaiming our Priestly Character* is one of the first in a series books to be published by IPF Publications intended to help foster renewal in the presbyterate for the good of the Church of the new millennium.

Rev. David L. Toups, S.T.D.
Solemnity of Mary, Mother of God
January 1, 2008

Associate Director of the Secretariat of
Clergy, Consecrated Life and Vocations
United States Conference of Catholic Bishops
Washington, D.C.

Notes

1 The new republication of *Christ the Ideal of the Priest* (San Francisco: Ignatius Press, 2005) will be used through out this text (cf. pg. 57 [49]). The numbers in brackets refer to an older edition that is still on the shelves of many priests (cf. *Christ the Ideal of the Priest*, trans. Matthew Dillon, O.S.B., 3rd ed. [London: Sands & Co., 1952]). I discovered the beauty of Marmion's writings in the course of my research and hence the title of my doctorate was: *The Sacerdotal Character as the Foundation of the Priestly Life: Including the Contribution of Blessed Columba Marmion*. The republication of his writings will be a source of renewal for many priests.

2 *Agere sequitur esse* is a principle of scholastic thought. This axiom, as presently applied to the priesthood, expresses the importance of proper knowledge of who one is in order to function or do what one is called to do (cf. *Summary of Scholastic Principles*, ed. Loyola University Associates [Chicago: Ability Press, 1951], 22; *ST* I, q. 85, a. 4 and *ST* I, II, q. 55, a. 2, *ad* 1).

Prologue

The past half century has brought enormous transformation in the life of the Church. Among the shifts that have occurred, seminary formation has undergone considerable upheaval since the mid-twentieth century, as has the image and role of the ordained priesthood. As a result, priests within a given presbyterate may identify with a variety of moments in the evolutionary convulsions that have marked the recent decades. In admittedly unjustly broad strokes, it appears that older members of the clergy, those nearest retirement age, received their education amid a period of ecclesiastical and theological stability as well as clear, precise descriptions of the priestly office and the life it entailed. Priests were revered authority figures who were distinguished by a special power to celebrate the sacraments. Another group of priests, those today most likely in positions of leadership as pastors and chancery personnel in dioceses, navigated a seminary experience during an era of shifting paradigms, innovative theological exploration, social mistrust of institutionalized authority, precipitous declines in both vocations and participation in the sacraments, and a focus on priesthood centered around activity such as preaching, care of the poor, or building community.

These two trends have been succinctly labeled the cultic model and the servant-leader model of priesthood respectively. It should be noted that neither group embraced a perception of priesthood in opposition to the other so much as each identifies most readily with the environment in which their vocations were received and formed.

A third group, the most recently ordained, presents an apparent resurgence of concern for clearly defined theological categories, a preoccupation with strict observance of magisterial statements, and an affinity for more traditional forms of piety and styles of worship. The newly ordained today arrive from a milieu predominated by contradictions. These young priests discerned the call to priestly service within a culture that seems in many ways antithetical to spirituality and openly hostile to a life commitment, particularly one involving celibacy. At the same time, they experienced a seminary system characterized by structure, theological rigor, and clearly articulated expectations of the priesthood. Much of this development can be attributed to the prodigious papacy of Pope John Paul II, whose letter, *Pastores Dabo Vobis*, has become the manual for seminary formation around the world, along with his many reflections on priesthood. Understandably, priests within a diocese may feel tensions, even conflicts, with one another as these different points of view collide in the day-to-day practice of ministry. Not so rare is the complaint of both pastors and their newly ordained associates that the other is far from where he ought to be theologically and pastorally. Divisions are emerging around the basic presuppositions of who the priest is and what he does. Reconciling such disparate positions in practice can be frustrating, acrimonious, and disruptive to parish communities.

Equipped with empirical data from recent studies comparing cross-generational clergy opinions, Father David Toups delves into the current situation, highlighting the relationship between retention rates of priests and confidence in the priestly character. *Reclaiming Our Priestly Character* provides a compelling exposition of the theology of the sacerdotal character as it has emerged in the Catholic theological tradition across the centuries. This is an illuminating, comprehensive survey of this aspect of the effect of ordination. Most appealing of all, this book may serve to ease the tensions between the different generations of priests today. A contemporary investigation of this character may provide the focus around which priests can identify and affirm what they have in common.

The appeal to the priestly character serves as the point of integration for all of priestly life in several ways. First, the exciting rediscovery of the permanent character received in priestly ordination functions as a theological and personal anchor for the ordained as a force of constancy amid the ever-evolving demands with which the priest is buffeted. While the number of priests in relation to the number of Catholics has declined dramatically, and the sexual abuse scandal has fomented cynicism among the laity, the public role of the priest and the esteem in which he is held have been considerably altered from what they once were. Diocesan priests today can anticipate a far different lifestyle than forty or fifty years ago. The priestly character reminds priests that they embrace fidelity to Jesus Christ and His Church, not as a job description but as a way of life. The seal impressed on the soul roots the priest in an interior reality rather than external details. This interior reality abides irrespective of changing life circumstances because it is a God-given gift that reflects the permanence of Christ's love for His Church.

Second, the indelible seal imparted at ordination reveals a point of balance between extreme positions. Perhaps the recovery of the theology of character can provide the integrating key to avoid a conception of priesthood that is too this worldly or too otherworldly. Neither the servant-leader model nor the cultic model is incorrect or sufficient on its own.

Third, reflection on the indelible character of the priesthood embraces both knowledge and affectivity. Within the theological discipline, one can intellectually assent to or deny a particular theological proposition, and this theological judgment will have implications for how one approaches further theological questions and practical circumstances. As *Reclaiming Our Priestly Character* amply demonstrates, reference to the priestly character largely receded in the wake of the Second Vatican Council and the ensuing effort to discover more original theological constructs. This book returns ontology to the fore, and Fr. Toups notes the apparent correlation between persistence in ministry and belief in the permanent character possessed by the ordained. Thus, statistical data confirms that an awareness of this theological import of the priestly character promotes greater fulfillment in ministry and reduces the likelihood of abandoning the priestly life. Knowledge forms behavior, yet knowledge alone does not suffice to engender saintliness.

Because the grace of the character reaches the man in the depths of his being, that is, at the level of ontology, this effect of ordination cannot be reduced simply to a theological truth to which one faithfully assents. This grace consumes a man's whole person and, therefore, cannot be spoken of only in terms of the intellect. Discussion of sacerdotal character ought to include the personal affective dimension, on which one bases priestly fidelity. Renewed attention to the priestly character as a theological concept does not automatically translate into more evident sanctity, even if statistical research suggests greater satisfaction or longevity in ministry among those who embrace the concept. The language of character unites the ontological reality articulated across the theological tradition with the free personal commitment of the priest to participate in the grace of ordination in ever expanding bounds of generosity. The ordination rite does not obliterate human freedom, which the ordained can direct equally toward self-interest as to self-sacrifice. This affective reception of the ontological gift makes possible a lively, loyal pastoral availability steadfastly rooted in Christ's own compassionate love for His people. It manifests itself in the deepening assimilation of the priest's freedom, intentionality, desires, attitudes, and affect into the very heart of the Risen Savior. The reception of ordination begs the priest each day to choose personal communion with the eternal High Priest as the central, irreplaceable, inviolable relationship of the priest's life.

In his valuable text, *Quickening the Fire in Our Midst*, Fr. George Aschenbrenner, S.J., coins the phrase presumption for perseverance and permanence to mark the individual surrender to the personal dimension of priestly life. The presumption blossoms forth as the fruit of a serious discernment focused on the movements of God's grace felt as a unique and unrepeatable plan for this man drawn to Holy Orders. Through a searching discernment, the candidate has sifted out the misleading tugs of self-interest and the always corrosive distortions with which the spirit of evil infects the human heart. So purified, the seminarian places before the Trinity his heart's desire clarified in the light of the Spirit, so that God may confirm the decision at hand. This careful process reverences the fact that one's identity and mission in vocation are God-given. Even prior to ordination, the candidate lives within the boundaries of priesthood and practices the virtues essential to integrated priestly holiness.

Notice that the presumption occurs before the priestly character has been received in ordination and prior to the candidate's exercise of sacramental ministry. The beauty of the presumption appears in the seminarian's interior peacefulness as he resolves to fashion every aspect of his life around the lifelong commitment to Jesus Christ as a priest. It manifests the subjective dispositions for a free and generous offering of self in surrender to the grace that God confers at ordination. The presumption declares the seminarian's renunciation of whatever may interfere with the fruitful participation in Christ's priesthood, even to a posture of detachment toward future temptations not yet perceived. It is a claim of priority in one's life, a priority of the bond with Jesus now and for the entirety of one's life. It pushes one beyond the comfortable, peaceful, or enthusiastic feelings of the present moment to consideration of frustration, disappointment, or resistance in the future without any withdrawal of the original self-offering to God. The presumption for perseverance and permanence takes seriously the meaning of the sacramental seal and its implications for the one who receives it. It indicates a profound willingness not only to be ontologically configured to Christ so as to be empowered to administer the sacraments but also to allow this configuration to radiate outwardly in a life radically patterned after the Good Shepherd at every level. The presumption recognizes that ordained ministry is the gift of God, but a gift that requires a lifelong personal response, an ever-deepening participation in the mystery of Trinitarian love.

In the life of the Christian, even more so in the case of a priest, the relationship with the Triune God is foundational. In fact, one does not really choose to seek ordination; rather, a man freely embraces priesthood out of obedience to the Spirit drawing one to a particular life of service in the Church and a particular way of incarnating Christ's faithful love for His people. It is an act of self-surrender realized within a posture of profound interior detachment, "Not my will, but Yours be done" (Lk 22:42). One prefers and yields to in joy whatever pleases the Father. It is the pleasing of the Father, not primarily the action of the priestly ministry, that is the source of priestly happiness and nourishment. By placing the basis of priestly character in the relationship between the ordained man and the Lord, one avoids the misconception of character as something external that is supernaturally imposed on the ordinand, like a mold. Instead, like the encounter with the Risen Jesus at Baptism or the reception of the Holy Spirit in Confirmation, the grace of Orders is always personal.

The intent here is to describe character as placing the recipient in a particular kind of relationship before the Father and with the Son to evidence the kenotic love of the Trinity in a unique way. The love of God, that is Christ, poured into the Church and embodied in a mysterious way by the priest, effects the Eucharist; the priest is the instrument of this Eucharistic mystery, not its cause. Even so, the gift of the indelible seal is not restricted only to the priest's sacramental role. The grace of the character means that the priest hosts a divine love in every interaction and relationship of his life, and he can cooperate with or frustrate this energy of self-offering. Without any insincere romanticism, one can say that the priest truly lives Christ's love. As one sacramentally configured to Christ, who has made himself both priest and sacrifice, the ordained participates specifically in Christ's own priestly love for humanity.

If there is a particularity to the priest's relationship with God, then there is a concomitant particularity to the priest's relationship with the Church. The historical emergence of the concept of the character conferred at ordination suggests a grace given by God, not so much for the priest personally as for the good of the Church. Ex opere operato serves the indefectibility of the sacramental life of the Church more than the personal sanctification of the priest as a man, although the priest's personal holiness is intimately bound up with the fruitful exercise of his ministry. Attention to the priestly character emerges from questions concerning the moral failure of individual priests and the consequence of personal lapses on the sacraments such a priest celebrates. The theological understanding of the priestly character guarantees the efficacy of the sacramental action as distinct from the moral perfection of the individual who presides over the ritual. In a real way, it seems as though the theological development of the character implies that God instituted priesthood for the benefit of those who are served and not primarily for the benefit of the one who administers the sacraments. A detrimental imbalance lurks in this description of character if one reduces the permanent character simply to divine deputation to officiate at sacramental rites, as though priesthood merely represents a function in the Church on the one hand. On the other hand, one must recognize that ordination places one at the service of God and Church, never to sanction an autonomous priestly class within the Church. Both extremes invariably warp an authentic ecclesiology.

In examining the relationship of the priest to the Church through the lens of the priestly character, it is evident that the use of the term develops primarily from situations of controversy, but more positive implications of this aspect of sacramental theology may be spun out in the present time as the awareness of the character has become well-established in the theological tradition. To say that the character exists in the service of the whole Church is to say, in other words, that God makes of the priest a gift to the Church by the event of ordination.

One can say that the priest submits his life to the grace of this character, deliberately speaking of his life, not simply his work or his ministry. The divine grace envelops the person of the priest in his most profound depths and precludes an impoverishing reduction of priesthood to a set of functions that he performs on specific occasions. Nor can the candidate for ordination be content with learning theological positions or perfecting rubrics. At ordination, the man's life enters a new phase of sacramentality. Whether baptizing, preaching, praying the Liturgy of the Hours, grocery shopping, exercising, visiting friends, or listening to music, the priest is a living symbol of Jesus' priestly fidelity to the Church. No details of the priest's life are excluded from configuration to Christ. Incarnate self-offering love animates every moment of priestly life. This conformity to Christ surpasses a cliché mindset: what would Jesus do? It assumes both an exterior and an interior configuration to the eternal High Priest. Visibly the priest strives to manifest evangelic virtue iconic of Christian service. Beneath the surface, in the sifting psychological and spiritual movements hidden from view, the priest seeks to acquire as his own the attitudes, desires, and motives of the Savior. A priest lives humbly with the responsibility that while the ontological mark is permanent, its outward manifestation can be distorted by his free will. The bread that is transformed at the words of consecration remains the Body of Christ once the liturgy has concluded. One cannot unmake the Eucharistic presence, but it can be defiled by acts of sacrilege. Similarly, ordination obligates the priest to reverence the grace of ordination by striving to express externally, through his own humanity, the bond he shares with Jesus Christ in his being.

While the sacramental moment of Orders occurs with the imposition of hands by the Bishop, the sacrament must be enfleshed in a day-to-day engagement of the grace received. Each sacrament involves an object, a richly polyvalent symbol that announces a deeper mystery. The person of the priest is such a symbol, and the theology of the character opens the imagination to perceive the mysterious truth sacramentally represented in priesthood. There is no priesthood without flesh. This is as true of Christ as for the Church today. Christ's priesthood exists because the Word has become incarnate. Priesthood continues in the Church because men have been ordained, and their human presence as sacrament discloses the mystery of paschal love in the Trinity, regardless of whether the priest is presiding in a sacramental role at any given moment. The sacramentality of his priesthood is continuous.

If an ordained man desires to live out the sacramental reality that has become his life, then there are specific steps he can take to reinforce the commitment of his personal freedom to the grace given him. It might be more accurate to imagine these behaviors not so much as methods but as integral dispositions or habits constitutive of sound, spiritual well-being as nutrition is to good physical health. The term dispositions resonates with special force here because it conveys the sense of interior allegiance, desire, and inclination more so than particular actions that are routinely fulfilled. It is this interior free movement of personal, loyal attachment to Christ that forms the seedbed from which the Spirit will produce abundant fruit. Lacking the interior passion for Christ and His Church, the one who observes even a sophisticated prayer regimen can lapse into ineffectual rote recitation or self-focused reflection. In practice, the discipline of prayer and the interior affections relate dialectically. Prayer arises from a heart aflame with love for the Lord, and it also intensifies that love as the soul rests in awed awareness of the Trinity. Underlying any real growth in intimate friendship with God is an enduring quality of receptivity. All grace is gift. Although once ordained the man remains a priest forever, in a profound way the priest is always receiving his priesthood from God.

First among the dispositions that promote fidelity to the Eternal Priest is the practice of discernment of spirits. Again, disposition is the appropriate word because discernment of spirits presupposes that one wants always to seek the voice of the Master and to exercise an eager willingness to respond to His call. As a set of skills or repeated practice only, discernment of spirits never fully transcends psychology or self-help. The essential component of mature, authentic discernment of spirits is the desire to remain an unwavering disciple of Jesus, Who is the Way, the Truth, and the Life. Authentic discernment of spirits ensures that one never separates personal contemplation from lived prayer; thus, ones actions assume the character of worship of God.

A second disposition that reinforces fidelity to the priestly character is a pattern of Scripture-based prayer. Attentiveness to the Word reminds the ordained that his priesthood is not his own but emanates from Christ's own self-sacrificing love. Returning repeatedly to the Word for nourishment, inspiration, and insight sustains the heart in receptivity. Its fruitfulness comes from listening. Praying with Scripture differs from study of Scripture in the sense that prayer opens one to an encounter with Christ as a person relevant to life now. The living Word that longs to be received invites one to step away from corrosive narcissism or paralyzing timidity and to be immersed in the holiness of God. It is in Scripture where over and over one discovers anew the splendid desires of the Trinity. If the priest does not allow the inspired text to penetrate his own spirit frequently, then he risks becoming untethered from the very source of his priestly identity. Distraction from the relationship with the Triune God will inevitably dilute the integrity of one's identity and thus undermine the fruitfulness of pastoral ministry. Scripture-based prayer as a disposition for priestly life fosters humility, for people justly expect that when the priest evangelizes, they will hear Jesus. The priest's frequent retreat in prayerful solitude into Christ's life, death, and resurrection reinforces his attachment to Christ in whose power he serves at the altar and in the world.

The third disposition that fortifies a priest's fidelity to the grace of ordination is a commitment to ongoing formation. The disposition interiorized through self-motivated, lifelong formation is the attitude of the pilgrim on the journey to the heavenly kingdom. The pilgrim rests but does not lose sight of the overall destination. Similarly, the priest seeks opportunities for ongoing growth that include but are not limited to education. The comparison is sometimes made between seminary formation and the apostles' companionship with Jesus during His public ministry. By sharing friendship with the Lord, listening to His words addressed to them as to the crowds, witnessing His miracles, submitting to His direction over their lives, sharing in His own prayer, and preaching the kingdom in His name, the twelve gradually assume Jesus' attitudes and desires. Truly they allow themselves to be formed in their whole persons. This participation in companionship with Jesus does not end when He is taken from them at the Ascension. In His Spirit's immediacy in their hearts, they continue a deep, personal loyalty to the Master, as well as increasing insight and affection.

Ongoing formation entails a communal dimension. Presbyterates grow through a positive exchange across generations of priests and through a friendly collaboration in the service with which God has charged them. Evidence suggests that priests are becoming more polarized by age and theological perspective. If this is accurate, stereotyping priests into categories invariably divides presbyterates and thwarts the good fruit that God intends. Opportunities for priests to develop friendships with other priests beyond their own peer group promote a greater likelihood of priests respecting one another and embracing a common identity. Priests share both the universal call to holiness and the sacramental configuration to Christ.

Finally, ongoing formation includes a reverent attention to the interior life. This means more than faithfulness to daily Mass and the Liturgy of the Hours. Through spiritual direction maintained over a lifetime and annual substantive retreat experiences, the priest engages in a true pilgrimage into the unfathomable depths of God's being-for-him. One does not make this journey in solitude; rather, he enjoys the blessed companionship of the Church in the persons of spiritual directors, confessors, and retreat masters.

Reclaiming Our Priestly Character, which is offered at a critical point in the Church's life, holds up the theology of the priestly character as a credible center for greater unity and balance in priesthood today. This text fits well into a broader movement of spiritual renewal within diocesan priesthood in a period of dramatic, often traumatic, change in the Church. Fr. Toups provides a valuable, thoughtful contribution to the discussion about contemporary priestly life; however, further conversation is warranted to flesh out more clearly the implications for safeguarding the spiritual vitality of priests. People should receive this work as an invitation to mine the tradition further and write more extensively about the interrelationship between the grace of ordination and the daily life of priests. This book gives momentum to this movement by offering a fresh examination of an ancient teaching that casts greater light on the present moment. Reflection and discussion around this topic could bridge some differences among clergy. More importantly, a closer look into the theology of the sacrament of Holy Orders may heal symptoms of fragmentation within contemporary priestly life. Significantly, the emphasis on the character imparted at ordination highlights the indispensable link to Jesus Christ. For the priest, this unique connection to the High Priest continues after ordination and summons within the priest a continuous, free, personal response. Indeed, the traditional term character points to a relationship with God that determines one's identity and mission as priest. Pope Benedict XVI, then Cardinal Joseph Ratzinger, speaking of the challenge of maintaining balance in priestly life, observes: "The foundation is an intimate communion with Christ whose food was to do the will of the Father (John 4:34). It is important that the ontological union with Christ abide in the conscience and in action: all that I do, I am doing in communion with Him. By doing it, I am with Him. All my activities, no matter how varied and often externally divergent, constitute only one vocation: to be together with Christ acting as an instrument in communion with Him."

Rev. James Rafferty

Fr. Rafferty, ordained in 1993, is a priest of the Diocese of Scranton. He has been actively involved in the programs of the Institute for Priestly Formation since 2003. Having served as a parish priest and a university chaplain, he is currently completing his doctoral studies in moral theology at the *Alphonsianum* in Rome.

Notes

1 George Aschenbrenner, SJ, *Quickening the Fire in Our Midst: The Challenge of Diocesan Priestly Spirituality* (Chicago: Loyola Press, 2002), 68-81. Cf. also Richard Gabuzda, "Relationship, Identity, Mission: A Proposal for Seminary Formation," in *Interiority for Mission: Spiritual Formation for Priests of the New Evangelization—Fourth Annual Symposium on the Spirituality and Identity of the Diocesan Priest*, 3-6 March 2005 (Omaha, Nebraska: Institute for Priestly Formation, 2006), 44. Fr. Gabuzda, Director of the Institute for Priestly Formation, underscores the interrelationship between relationship, identity, and mission.

2 Cardinal Joseph Ratzinger, "Life and Ministry of Priest," in *Priesthood: A Greater Love—International Symposium on the Thirtieth Anniversary of the Promulgation of the Conciliar Decree Presbyterorum Ordinis*, 28 October 1995 (Philadelphia: Archdiocese of Philadelphia, 1997), 126.

Chapter 1

Reclaiming Character:

The Solid Foundation of the Doctrine of Priestly Character

To reclaim its distinctively priestly character, it is helpful for the presbyterate to understand the history and tradition of this character in the Church. Following the Thomistic axiom *agere sequitur esse* – priests who know their identity are more likely to live as they are called. Knowledge in this case is foundational for the entire living out of the priestly vocation. Ten years after the Second Vatican Council, now Cardinal, Albert Vanhoye, S.J., wrote: "If they do not wish to wander in wrong directions, priests must, first of all, be sure of the doctrinal basis of their vocation."[1]

The proper perception of the sacramental character of orders helps priests to live and fulfill their pastoral duties (*orthopraxis*), since *orthodoxy* leads to *orthopraxis*. Pope

Benedict XVI, then Cardinal Ratzinger, affirmed: "For the early Christians, there was no difference between what is today often distinguished as orthodoxy and orthopraxis, as right doctrine and right action."[2] Thus it is important to be grounded in both right doctrine and, by God's grace, its subsequent response, right action. St. Thomas Aquinas advises, "Nothing can be done aright [...] except in so far as is previously directed by the knowing reason."[3]

Proper knowledge is relevant for structuring proper living. The priest must know that the gift received at ordination permanently marks his soul and draws him into a unique union with Jesus Christ the Head and Shepherd of the Church. The priest's union with the High Priest is so profound it is ontological. "This special participation in Christ's priesthood does not disappear even if a priest, for ecclesial or personal reasons, is dispensed or removed from the exercise of his ministry" (*UT* 11).[4] The *Catechism* states:

> It is true that some validly ordained can, for grave reasons, be discharged from the obligations and functions linked to ordination, or can be forbidden to exercise them; but he cannot become a layman again in the strict sense, because the character imprinted by ordination is forever. The vocation and mission received on the day of his ordination mark him permanently (*CCC* 1583).

This book does not intend to offer an exhaustive presentation of the Church's teaching regarding the sacramental character of the ministerial priesthood but to offer a sufficiently robust overview of this theology by looking at the Scriptures, the Tradition of the Church, and Magisterial documents. The doctrine regarding the unique nature of the priesthood is sound and true and has been consistently reaffirmed by the Church throughout the centuries.

Biblical Foundations

A number of scriptural citations and expressions have helped the Church in the formulation of the doctrine of the priestly character. Throughout the Gospels, the actions of Christ and the Apostles lay the foundation for Holy Orders. Likewise, the theology of the priesthood is found in expressions like the "laying on of hands" and *sphragis*. Sacred Scripture is the *norma normans non normata*[5] for all further theological development, and some of the early Church practices recorded in Scripture help lay the foundation for the development of the doctrine of priestly character.

It is evident from the Sacred Scriptures that Jesus Himself intended the apostolic ministry to continue. Fr. Jean Galot, S.J., noted:

> It is important to insist that Jesus willed a succession marked by historical continuity with Himself and with the group of the Twelve, for to this group He handed over the totality of priestly power. [...] He bestows priestly power only through a chain of historical transmission in which the Twelve are the first link.[6]

Jesus knew the end of the world was not to come immediately, as evidenced in His call to proclaim the Gospel to the ends of the earth (Mk. 13:9-10 and Mt. 28:18-20), and that this end would not come until this task had been accomplished (Mt. 24: 14). This mission would require successors to carry out the command to teach "Jesus Christ, and him crucified" and risen from the dead (cf. 1 Cor. 2:2 and 15:4), to preach the Gospel to all peoples, and to fulfill the particularly priestly role instituted at the Last Supper: "Do this in memory of me" (Lk. 22:19). The witness of the Scriptures is clear that it was Jesus' intent that this ministry be continued.

The practice of the early Church points to the passing on of the ministry entrusted to the Apostles. It is evident in Acts that the Apostles certainly intended to hand on to other disciples a spiritual gift for the continuation of their ministry in the early Church. This is first seen in the election of Matthias to succeed the in office of Apostle, the seat of Judas (Acts 1:15-26). In addition, Acts 6, is sometimes regarded as the first written account of an "ordination" performed by the Apostles.[7] The Apostles evidently felt it within their authority to continue, transmit, and "appoint to this office."[8] The intention to transmit the office showed a real awareness that the authority of Christ had been entrusted to them and was thus meant to be passed on in the Church. The New Testament points, even if only implicitly at times, to the "change" which has occurred in the minister to whom the sacred office has been bestowed. Apostolic succession and the character intimately linked to it are not simply a replacing of the Twelve, but the continuance of their ministry of spreading the Good News as commanded by Christ. These successors were to transmit faithfully the message both in word and deed and to hand on the traditions and teachings of Christ and the Apostles: "I received from the Lord what I also handed on to you..." (1 Cor. 11:23).

The continuity of the apostolic ministry gave assurance to the early Christian community that the ministry of Christ would perdure. The gift of succession was passed on through the "imposition of hands" by the Apostles and their successors. St. Paul, especially in his letters to Timothy, enjoins this new *presbyteros/episkopos*[9] to recognize the gift he has received: "I admonish you to stir into flame the gift of God bestowed when my hands were laid on you" (2 Tim. 1:6). Since the earliest times, the "imposition of hands" has been the sign of imparting the Spirit to the recipient.[10] Priesthood, or the office of presbyter,[11] is a gift from God communicated by the Holy Sprit through prayer and the laying on of hands by the Apostles and their successors.

> Do not neglect the gift you have, which was conferred on you through the prophetic word with the imposition of hands of the presbyterate. Be diligent in these matters, be absorbed in them, so that your progress may be evident to everyone. Attend to yourself and to your teaching; persevere in both tasks, for by doing so you will save both yourself and those who listen to you (1 Tim. 4:14-16).

These two Pauline texts have been used traditionally to point to the moment of ordination for the recipient, Timothy. As one commentator wrote:

> If we must hold as correct the exegesis that comments on the effect of Paul's imposition of hands on Timothy (we hold that it really

> does mean Ordination, that the charism is
> permanent) we note that this imposition
> of hands produces a charism which can be
> neglected and revived, which must be guarded
> but may be left inactive and yet persists so that
> we can always appeal to it, this must mean
> that Paul's imposition of hands gives a charism
> which cannot be identified with habitual
> grace nor with a simple series and sum total of
> special actual graces.[12]

When St. Paul speaks of "fanning into flame," he seems to be writing of a permanent reality residing within Timothy that can be re-vivified if it has been neglected.

Terminology pointing to the permanence of the ministry passed on through the imposition of hands is also another relevant consideration. One such term is *sphragis* (σφραγις).[13] The scriptures refer to being "sealed (σφραγισαμενος) by the power of the Holy Spirit" in order to fulfill certain functions within the Church.[14] The *Catechism of the Catholic Church* makes reference to the seal, even using the Greek alliteration, "the image of the seal (*sphragis*) has been used by some theological traditions to express the indelible 'character' imprinted by [the] three unrepeatable sacraments" (*CCC* 698). Through the passage of time, the two words, "seal" and "character," will be used almost interchangeably denoting the permanency of the sacraments of Baptism, Confirmation, and Holy Orders.

The actual word "character" is a *hapax legomenon*, that is, it appears only once in the New Testament, in the Letter to the Hebrews (1:3). In the *Septuagint* this word is used only three times.[15] The Hebrew word that it translates means: to burn or scorch, or even a scab or a scar.[16] This imagery helps the understanding of the permanence of the character – like a scar that remains. "In Greek, a *character* was analogous to a *sphragis*: it meant initially whatever 'produces' an imprint, and then the 'imprint' itself. In Latin, the ineffaceable tattoo a soldier received when enlisting was called either a *signaculum*, or a *character*."[17] The Greek word itself comes from everyday usage for an "engraving tool" or a "die stamp" in order to mark one's possessions.[18] For instance, note the following usage of Hebrews 1:3: "This Son is the reflection of the Father's glory, the *exact representation* (*character*/χαρακτηρ) of the Father's being, and he sustains all things by his powerful word."[19] This might also be translated, "the express image of God's person" or in another translation, the "very stamp of his nature."[20] Though it is used only once, and in reference to Christ, one can see how this word-image will be used to express that which is possessed by the men who stand *in persona Christi capitis*.

While the New Testament establishes the foundations upon which the Church's theology flows, some are critical of over-historicizing scriptural accounts. However, even among scholars with a more critical view of the "historical lineage" of apostolic succession, this view still affirmed that the "intention" of Christ was to have this ministry continue. As Fr. Raymond Brown, S.S., explained the difficulties of tracing the ritual and juridical beginnings of the priesthood, he maintained:

> Such a picture of the development of the Christian priesthood must of necessity modify our understanding of the claim that historically Jesus instituted the priesthood

at the Last Supper. This statement is true to the same real but nuanced extent as the statement that the historical Jesus instituted the Church. By selecting followers to take part in the proclamation of God's kingdom, Jesus formed the nucleus of what would develop into a community and ultimately into the Church. By giving special significance to the elements of the (Passover?) meal that he ate with his disciples on the night before he died, Jesus supplied his followers with a community rite that would ultimately be seen as a sacrifice and whose celebrants would hence be seen as priests.[21]

Donald Wuerl, now Archbishop of Washington, D.C., stressed in his early book on the priesthood:

A gradual development or clarification of priestly functions does not mean that such functions came into being later in the life of the Church. When we state that the designation by name of a particular office required time, we are not necessarily saying that the office and work do not exist from the beginning of the life of the Church.[22]

St. Paul showed that this ministry was passed on through the "laying on of hands," conferring a spiritual gift, as the Church would later come to understand, which marks the soul permanently. The seal (σφραγις) binds the minister to Christ in order to stand in His very Person and continue the ministry He began through His Apostles. Fr. Aiden Nichols, O.P., explains:

> What we should say is [...] that the apostles,
> in instituting local ordained ministries for
> the good order of the communities they had
> founded, necessarily conceived such ministry
> as involving good order in cultic presidency,
> teaching and pastoral discipline, since these
> are the constitutive elements of the Church's
> common life.[23]

The successors of the Apostles have been called, permanently
sealed, and sacramentally configured to Christ to teach, govern,
and sanctify since the time of the apostolic Church. An appraisal
of the priesthood in the early Church positions the doctrinal
development of the notion of the sacramental character in its
proper context. In selecting this method, the theology behind
apostolic succession will prove to be a central foundation for the
understanding of the sacramental character of the priesthood.

The Early Church

In the post-apostolic period, the early Fathers of the
Church do not yet speak in explicit terms about the sacramental
character of Holy Orders. The notion of "character" as such
will be developed later in history, but the teaching is certainly
implicitly present in the writings of the early Fathers of the
Church as they developed the notion of the "seal of baptism"
together with a greater understanding of the dignity of the
priesthood. The early Church saw the sacerdotal office (proper
to bishops and priests) as something that is essential to the life
of the faithful; therefore, this ministry must be guaranteed and

validated through ordination which becomes binding on the recipient. The sacramental theology of the "mark" given at Baptism provided the theological insight and understanding of the sacerdotal character. By making the analogy with Baptism, the Fathers eventually arrived at an analogous theology for Holy Orders.

The third successor of St. Peter in Rome was Clement. St. Clement was not only chronologically close to the time of the Apostles, but St. Irenaeus believed that he was personally acquainted with both Saints Peter and Paul.[24] Clement, bishop of Rome from 92 to 101, wrote to the Church in Corinth around the year 96.[25] In this letter he explains how the "office" of apostle is handed down through the ministry of the bishop.

> Our apostles also knew, through our Lord Jesus Christ, [that] there would be strife on account of the office of the episcopate. For this reason, therefore, inasmuch as they had obtained a perfect fore-knowledge of this, they appointed those [ministers] already mentioned, and afterwards gave instructions, that when these should fall asleep, other approved men should succeed them in their ministry.[26]

St. Clement's intention is to stress that the "apostles provided for an orderly succession for the ministry they established."[27] The theme of Pope Clement's letter is "clearly Church ministry, and more precisely, [...] the theme of succession in Church ministry."[28] The passing on of the sacred and sacerdotal office is evident in the immediate post-apostolic period. The ministry is based upon a sure apostolic succession. The man holding this office cannot be easily dismissed; already there seems to be a sense of permanence being formulated by the early Church.

St. Ignatius of Antioch (+107) wrote of the essential roles of the presbyters and the bishop as the hierarchy (i.e. "sacred-ordering") of the community.[29] In his *Letter to the Smyrnaeans*, St. Ignatius reminded the community that everything they do, whether it be baptizing or celebrating the Eucharist, must be done under the authority of the bishop "so that everything that is done may be secure and valid."[30]

St. Irenaeus of Lyon (140-202) indicated clearly that it is essential to be connected to the apostolic Church because it ensures a connection to Christ Himself. In his work, *Against Heresies,* he wrote:

> Wherefore it is incumbent to obey the presbyters who are in the Church – those who, as I have shown, possess the succession from the Apostles; those who, together with the succession of the episcopate, have received the certain gift of truth (*charisma veritatis certum*), according to the good pleasure of the Father.[31]

Fr. Francis Sullivan, S.J., in his book, *From Apostles to Bishops*, commented on this text: "Irenaeus insisted that only by listening to those who maintained this 'original succession' could one be assured of hearing the truth taught by the apostles."[32] Fr. Jean-Hervé Nicolas, O.P., explained that this text refers specifically to the sacramental character and to the indefectibility, or assurance, of the validity of the sacraments as expressed by Irenaeus, *charisma veritatis certum.*[33] Apostolic succession ensures the transmission of the sacramental character and permanent nature of Holy Orders. For the Fathers of the first two centuries after Christ, it was imperative to follow what had been passed down from the Apostles and their successors. Therefore, apostolic succession confirms that the ministers are not acting in their own name or of their own authority but in the very name and authority of Christ Himself.

Tertullian (160-222/3) wrote *The Prescription Against Heretics* around the year 200,[34] conveying the false practices of the heretics and revealing their heretical disciplines. With regard to their "priests" he wrote of their disbelief in the permanence of the office: "today he is a presbyter who tomorrow is a layman."[35] By contrasting unorthodox practices with those of the Church, Tertullian emphasized the permanence of orders in the way the Church views the office. There is no sense of "changeability" in this particular ministerial vocation in the Church.

St. Hippolytus, a prolific writer from the beginning of the third century in Rome, described and recorded the rites of ordination for bishops, priests, and deacons. One of his works, *The Treatise on the Apostolic Tradition*,[36] demonstrates that these rituals were already part of the tradition of the Church in Rome by the end of the second century. He stressed the importance of apostolic succession and the profound dignity conferred on the priest through the "imposition of hands." Hippolytus wrote: "And when a presbyter is ordained (*cheirotonein*) the bishop shall lay his hand upon his head, the presbyters also touching him."[37] Regarding the ordination of presbyters as recorded by Hippolytus, it is noted:

> The main part of this prayer is petition for the
> individual being ordained; but it concludes
> with the request that God may grant 'the
> spirit of (His) grace, keeping it indefectible
> in us, and render us worthy, once filled with
> this spirit, to serve (Him) in simplicity of
> heart.'[38]

The prayer is for the apostolic ministry to continue through
the ordained, "keeping it indefectible." One cannot argue that
this citation is directly pointing to the permanent character of
the priesthood; however, it does suggest that, once ordained,
the man must live a life of service and sacramental ministry
for the community.

St. Hippolytus' use of the term "priesthood" (not
simply presbyter) in the ordination rite is important in the
development of the theology of the Sacrament of Holy Orders.
A distinction in terminology should be inserted here. Taken
from Christianity's Jewish roots, the word "priest" began
to be associated with the worship of the New Covenant.
Toward the end of the second century and into the third
century the word for "priest," *sacerdos* and *hiereus* (in Latin
and Greek respectively), is used to designate the bishop and
presbyter. They will become more and more interchangeable
with the passage of time, especially with the title presbyter.
This is because the bishop also retains a priestly office. This
is noted by Lee Bacchi: "Hippolytus' remark that deacons
are ordained not to the priesthood but to the ministry, may
indicate that Hippolytus included the presbyter as well as the
bishop in his conception of priesthood."[39] Showing how the
words became synonymous, Sr. Agnes Cunningham wrote:

The word *presbyteros* (presbyter) is clearly central to an understanding of the priesthood, as that concept developed in the patristic age. [...] At times, [*hiereus* (priest)] is synonymous with presbyter, although it was used to refer commonly to both *episkopoi* (bishops) and *presbyteroi* (presbyters) in the responsibilities of offering sacrifice and showing pastoral care.[40]

Fr. Coppens explains the development of these terms regarding the priesthood:

There is no doubt that the use of the terms *hierus* and *sacerdos* for the two higher degrees of the hierarchy became widespread at a relatively early date. [...] it does appear in the First Council of Constantinople. At first only the bishop is called *hiereus*. Later when he was given the title *archiereus* the simple term *hiereus* devolved upon the presbyter.[41]

Pope Benedict XVI, then as Cardinal Ratzinger, stated that "it is not enough to do the terminological research on the concepts of presbyter and *hiereus* (*sacerdos*) that were first separate and later on united."[42] To understand the priesthood, he explains, it must be seen in connection to the sacrifice.

By means of the sacrifice of Christ and of its acceptance in the resurrection, the whole cultic and priestly patrimony of the Old Testament was entrusted to the Church. [...] [T]he priesthood of the Church is the continuation and revival of the priesthood of the Old Testament, which finds its true accomplishment in the radical and transforming newness.[43]

The Church Fathers began to discuss in earnest the specifically sacramental character of the priesthood by making an analogy with the seal of baptism. "We note that the notion of a sacramental character derives from speculations on the σφραγις [*sphragis*] which go back to Christian antiquity and ended, it seems with a first attempt at systematization by St. Augustine."[44] Many of the Church Fathers wrote about the baptized having received "the seal" (σφραγιδα).[45] As a person was "sealed" by the Holy Spirit in Baptism, it was eventually deduced, a seal was also impressed upon the soul of the ordained. Because of the permanent nature and mission of the priesthood, this seal could never be removed.

The indelible nature of ordination was attested to at the First Ecumenical Council held in Nicaea in 325, emphasizing that even apostate priests are not re-ordained.[46] Fr. Garrigou-Lagrange, O.P., noted: "Even from the practice of not repeating ordination, much information can be gathered about the effects of this Sacrament, especially about the indelible character."[47]

Central figures in the patristic period regarding further development of the theology of the character are St. Gregory of Nazianzus, St. John Chrysostom, and St. Augustine of Hippo. St. Gregory of Nazianzus (329-389/90) developed his theology of the priesthood, understanding the "seal" as applied to the one dispensing the sacraments and not just the recipient of Baptism; the seal of Baptism was the paradigm. He addressed those who were worried about receiving the sacraments from unworthy ministers:

> Do not say, "I do not mind a mere Priest, if he is a celibate, and a religious, and of angelic

life; for it would be a sad thing for me to be
defiled even in the moment of my cleansing."
Do not ask for credentials of the preacher or
the baptizer. [...] Do not judge your judges,
you who need healing; and do not make nice
distinctions about the rank of those who shall
cleanse you, or be critical about your spiritual
fathers. One may be higher or lower than
another, but all are higher than you. Look at it
this way. One may be golden, another iron, but
both are rings and have engraved on them the
same royal image [*icon*]; and thus when they
impress wax, what difference is there between
the seal of one and that of the other? None.
Detect the material in the wax, if you are so
very clever. Tell me which is the impression of
the iron ring, and which is the golden. And
how do they come to be one? The difference
is in the material and not in the seal.[48]

The same sacrament is administered by a worthy minister
or by an unworthy one: "One may be golden, another iron,
but both are rings and have engraved on them the same royal
image." Thus there is no difference in the way the wax is
impressed. Each signet ring (i.e. the minister) has the capacity
to imprint the seal regardless of the material. The sacraments
are valid regardless of the worthiness of the one who performs
them. The priest, who has the "same royal image," is able to
dispense the sacraments because of something objectively
within him.

St. John Chrysostom (344-407) wrote of the
priesthood in terms of being an instrument of Christ: a vessel
through which Christ works efficaciously.[49] He reminded

the people in his homilies and writings that it is Christ who works through the hands of the priest. God works even through unworthy persons:

> Believe, therefore, that even now it is that supper, at which He Himself sat down. For this is in no respect different from that. [...] When therefore thou seest the priest delivering [the Eucharist] unto thee, account not that it is the priest that doeth so, but that it is Christ's hand that is stretched out."[50]

Chrysostom made clear that it is Christ working through the priest who is standing in His Person by virtue of ordination. Pointing to the theology of the sacramental character, Chrysostom stressed the validity of the sacraments because of the legitimacy of the priesthood. The sacraments are the same; Christ is the Priest. Through apostolic succession, Christ's Priesthood is shared.

Chrysostom wrote *On the Priesthood* in the latter part of the fourth century (ca. 387). Chrysostom reminded his reader that it is God who is acting through the priest; the power he possesses comes from above.

> For they who inhabit the earth and make their abode there are entrusted with the administration of things which are in Heaven, and have received an authority (*exousian*) which God has not given to angels or archangels. [...] But I see it all put into the hands of these men by the Son. For they have been conducted to this dignity (*metathentes*) as if they were already translated to Heaven, and had transcended human nature, and were

released from the passions to which we are liable. [...] For if no one can enter into the kingdom of Heaven except he be regenerate through water and the Spirit, and he who does not eat the flesh of the Lord and drink His blood is excluded from eternal life, and if all these things are accomplished only by means of those holy hands, I mean the hands of the priest, how will any one, without these, be able to escape the fire of hell, or to win those crowns which are reserved for the victorious?[51]

Priests certainly have not been freed from their human limitations with regard to their will and conscience; they do not cease to be human. But they have "received a power (*exousian*)" at their ordinations "elevating" them above the "nature" they possessed before. The word *exousia* comes from the two Greek roots: *ex* and *ousia*; literally "from one's very being." This is the word used in the New Testament in reference to Christ, Who "spoke with power and authority," (Lk. 4.32) which literally emanated from His Person. During the patristic period it began to be used to specifically refer to the "authority given to the apostles" and "episcopal and pastoral authority."[52] Chrysostom clearly recognized the priest was changed in his inmost being and used the term *metathentes*. The root of this word means "to effect a change in state or condition, to change or alter" and it is also used in Hebrews 7:12: "when the priesthood is changed, i.e. passed on to another."[53] This clearly points to the profound gift and radical transformation of the soul by virtue of the priestly ordination.

Consequently, Chrysostom also points to the great responsibility placed upon the shoulders of the priest to "live a life worthy of the calling" received by the Lord. Like other Fathers, his theology of Baptism was intimately connected to the scriptural idea of the soul being "marked" or "sealed." He then used the same analogy for the priesthood: the character assures the efficacy of the sacraments despite the worthiness of the priest. These two notions in the theology of Chrysostom were also clearly enunciated in the teachings of St. Augustine.

St. Augustine (354-430), bishop of Hippo, develops the theology of Orders beyond that of any of his contemporaries. "He used the word 'character' to describe the reality which underlies and helps explain the Church's belief and custom that Baptism, Confirmation and Orders are not repeated."[54] Augustine's contribution to the development and clarification of the Church's theology of the sacraments emerged as confusion and heresies arose, namely the Donatists. The priest, once marked by the character of Orders, is always a priest. Augustine wrote:

> Let him also consider the analogy of the military mark, which, though it can both be retained, as by deserters, and, also be received by those not in the army, yet ought not to be either received or retained outside its ranks; and, at the same time, it is not changed or renewed when a man is enlisted or brought back to his service.[55]

St. Augustine extends this analogy to the apostate priest who desires to repent and come back into full communion. One scholar, referring to St. Augustine's writings, explained it thus:

Just as baptism causes a real but invisible transformation of the recipient by means of external signs, so too, in ordination recipients are really inwardly transformed by sensible signs. Just as baptism imparts a character which cannot be effaced even if the recipient should choose to repudiate the Christian way of life, so too ordination permanently marks a human being, so that even if he does not exercise his order's function he remains configured to the order.[56]

During his controversy with the Donatists, Augustine wrote *Against the Letter of Parmenian*. Writing as a theologian, now Cardinal Walter Kasper explains the controversy:

[It] took place in the fifth century between Augustine and the Donatists with respect to the proper understanding of the holiness of the Church and its ministers. At that time the Church decided in favor of Augustine that the holiness of the ministry is not founded in the personal holiness of the minister – thus not in whether or not he carries out his praxis in a holy manner – but in the gift of grace and the commission that is given him by Jesus Christ in the Holy Spirit, which precedes his own activity, i.e., that is due him because of his "being."[57]

In this apologetical treatise, Augustine taught the unrepeatable nature of Baptism and Orders: "Both of these (*baptismus et ordo*) are Sacraments, and each is given to a man by a sacred rite, the one, when he is baptized, and the other when he is ordained. In the Catholic Church, therefore, it is not permitted to repeat either of these Sacraments."[58] He explained that those who repent and return to the Church are not re-baptized. If they were priests, they are not re-ordained because "their ordination remains whole (*ordinatio mansit integra*)."[59] The ordination remains whole (*integra*) because the character imparted on the soul is permanent. Because of the sacramental character, Augustine stressed the validity of the sacraments celebrated by a priest regardless of his worthiness. The theological expression developed in the Middle Ages, *ex opere operato*, comes from the Augustinian understanding of the sacramental life.[60] It means that the sacrament (or work) performed with correct form, matter, and intention is valid.

Some sixty-six years after Augustine's death, Pope Anastasius II, in 496, issued his first epistle, *Exordium Pontificatus mei*, regarding the validity of the sacraments administered by schismatic clergy. He wrote for the people to be at peace if they had received sacraments from a schismatic bishop.

> According to the most sacred custom of the Catholic Church, let the heart of your serenity acknowledge that no share in the injury from the name of Acacius should attach to any of these whom Acacius *the schismatic bishop* has baptized, or to any whom he has ordained priests or levites according to the canons, lest perchance the grace of the sacrament seem less powerful when conferred by an unjust [person]. ... For if the rays of that visible sun are not stained by contact with any pollution

when they pass over the foulest places, much less is the virtue of him who made that visible [sun] fettered by any unworthiness in the minister.

Therefore, then, this person [Acacius] has only injured himself by wickedly administering the good. For the inviolable sacrament, which was given through him, held the perfection of its virtue for others.[61]

Anastasius II affirmed that the sacraments indeed are valid despite the disposition of the minister. This supports both the integrity of the sacramental life of the Church "according to the most sacred custom" and the profound reality and power of the priestly character that is not altered by the priest's disposition.

During the period of the early Church, the development of liturgical prayers reveals the parallel development of doctrine: *Lex orandi, lex credendi.* The early rites of ordination point implicitly to the theology of the sacerdotal character. In the fifth century text, *Testamentum Domini*, an ordination rite based on the *Apostolic Traditions* of Hippolytus (third century), the Church in Syria makes reference to this doctrine, "[...] hear us, and turn toward this your servant, and make [him] a partaker and grant him the spirit of grace and of reason and of strength, [the] spirit of the presbyterate which does not age, indissoluble, homogenous [...]."[62] Evident in these earliest rites of ordination is the understanding that the priesthood is for the whole of life. Nothing in these prayers implies that the ministry of the priesthood is only for a period of time; rather permanence is explicit in the ordination rituals.[63]

The early Fathers of the Church[64] held that what priests possess within themselves by virtue of ordination was indeed something that transformed their inmost being and could not be repeated or erased. Using the analogy of the Eucharistic Bread that still appears to be bread but has been radically changed into the Body of Christ, St. Gregory of Nyssa writes:

> The bread again is at first common bread, but when the sacramental action consecrates it, it is called, and becomes, the Body of Christ. So with the sacramental oil; so with the wine: though before the benediction they are of little value, each of them, after the sanctification bestowed by the Spirit, has its several operations. The same power of the word, again, also makes the priest venerable and honorable, separated (*chorizomenon*) by the new blessing bestowed upon him, from his community with the mass of men. While but yesterday he was one of the mass, one of the people, he is suddenly rendered a guide, a president, a teacher of righteousness, an instructor in hidden mysteries; and this he does without being at all changed in body or in form; but, while continuing to be in all appearance the man he was before, being, by some unseen power and grace, transformed in respect of his unseen soul to the higher condition.[65]

Even though, at times, this understanding was only implicitly present, by the time of St. Augustine, this teaching became explicit. The Augustinian development elucidates that which was previously taught. Though in seminal form in the post-apostolic period, everything the Church was to become was already implicitly present.[66] As a result of the sacramental character, the priesthood ensures the validity of the sacraments being communicated to God's people. As seen below, this doctrine has continued to develop through theological precision and become clearer through the passage of time.

Medieval Period

Pope Innocent III, in his *Letter to Humbert, Archbishop of Arles* (1201), speaks, for the first time in any kind of formal or magisterial manner, of "the imprint of the Christian character" with regards to baptism.[67] This is an important step in the doctrinal development of sacramental theology because this terminology will soon be officially applied to the three sacraments of Baptism, Confirmation, and Holy Orders by the Magisterium of the Church.

St. Thomas Aquinas

St. Thomas Aquinas (1225-1274) takes the "seeds" of the theological thought from the Fathers, particularly of St. Augustine, expounds upon them, and deepens the Church's understanding of sacramental character. Other medieval theologians who contributed to this discussion are Peter Lombard, Alexander of Hales, Bonaventure, and John Duns Scotus.[68]

In the *Tertia Pars* of the *Summa Theologiae*,[69] Aquinas describes what and where the character is, reaffirms its permanent nature, and explains its purpose in God's plan of salvation; that is, by the character, the priest is given a *deputatio* and receives a spiritual power in order to do God's work *in persona Christi et Ecclesiae*. Aquinas asks the question: "Whether a Sacrament Imprints a Character on the Soul?"[70] He cites St. Paul (2 Cor. 1:21-22), stating that the Lord has "sealed us (*signavit nos*)," and then writes: "a character means nothing else than a kind of sealing."[71] This refers to the permanent nature of character. The whole of life is affected by this mark of possession.

Quoting St. Augustine (*Contra Parmenianum* 2, 13), Aquinas uses the analogy of a soldier who deserted the army and then desired to return to his duty. In order for him to return to service of the army, the character must simply be acknowledged or recognized, not redone. The character is a seal "imprinted on the soul" which cannot be erased. Citing Hebrews 1:3, "Christ is *the figure* or χαραχτήρ *of the substance of the Father*," Aquinas demonstrates that the character is a kind of assimilation of one thing to another.[72] As Christ is the image or imprint of the Father, so the Christian is assimilated into Christ's own image; His figure is imprinted on the soul. "[T]he eternal Character is Christ Himself [citing Heb. 1:3]. It seems, therefore, that the character should properly be attributed to Christ."[73] Christ is the Character or visible sign of God. "[Therefore, the] sacramental character is specifically the character of Christ, seeing that a configuration to his priesthood is imparted to the faithful through sacramental characters which are nothing else than a certain kind of

participation in the priesthood of Christ deriving from
Christ himself."[74] The character that is imprinted in the soul
is a participation in the priesthood of Christ. The character
is attributed to Christ; it is not Christ Himself. However,
because Christ's priesthood is eternal and cannot pass away,[75]
those who are given a participation in that priesthood through
sacramental configuration share in the eternity of the gift
received. Character cannot be lost, as St. Thomas writes:

> The reason of this is that the character is an
> instrumental power (*virtus instrumentalis*),
> as stated above (*ad* 1), and the nature of an
> instrument as such is to be moved by another,
> but not to move itself; this belongs to the
> will. Consequently, however much the will be
> moved in the contrary direction, the character
> is not removed (*characterem non removetur*),
> by reason of the immobility of the principal
> mover (*propter immobilitatem principalis
> moventis*).[76]

Despite how much the ordained man may struggle against
the fulfillment of his priestly vocation, St. Thomas writes
that the character is imparted on the intellectual power of
the soul,[77] and because, as Fr. Dillenschneider comments:

> "our intellect is incorruptible, the character
> which is inherent in it is equally incorruptible:
> '*Sicut intellectus perpetuus est et incorruptibilis,
> ita character indelebiliter manet in anima.*'
> One cannot kill his priestly character anymore
> than he can kill the intelligent soul."[78]

God Himself is the Unmoved Mover, and the man who has received the character enters into a permanent relationship with Him Who is unchangeable. Christ's Priesthood is eternal and cannot pass away; therefore, the priestly character will also remain eternally intact.[79] When Christ wills to make a person a priest at ordination, that act of the will does not change because Christ's priesthood cannot change. David Power, O.M.I., has commented:

> Thomas carefully distinguishes between the character and the grace of the sacrament, something which had not been done carefully enough by previous theologians. He does not divorce grace and character, because he shows that there must be a close connection between them, but his theology also shows that the power of the character does not depend upon grace for its operation and that it is not just a sign of grace, but rather of a configuration to Christ's priesthood, which allows participation in public worship.[80]

Since Christ's Priesthood is forever, those marked by His Priesthood cannot have that mark blotted out in this life or the life to come.

> Although external worship does not last after this life, yet its end remains. Consequently, after this life the character remains, both in the good as adding to their glory, and in the wicked as increasing their shame: just as the character of the military service remains in the soldiers after the victory, as the boast of the conquerors, and the disgrace of the conquered.[81]

The character will endure eternally either for glory or shame. St. Thomas affirmed that the mark is lasting and ultimately ordered to the worship of God in Heaven.

The purpose of the sacramental character[82] is ordered to divine worship in this life and in the next. The Christian is deputed (*deputatio ad cultum divinum*) to receive or to act in the sacramental life of the Church. The seal is imparted in order to function in the Christian life, particularly in *cultum divinum*.[83] Only three sacraments "depute a man to do or receive something pertaining to the worship of the priesthood of Christ" and only those three cannot be repeated.[84]

> But it is the Sacrament of Order that pertains to the sacramental agents; for it is by this sacrament that men are deputed to confer sacraments on others: while the sacrament of Baptism pertains to the recipients, since it confers on man the power to receive the other sacraments of the Church; whence it is called the *door of the sacraments*. In a way Confirmation also is ordained for the same purpose [...]. Consequently, these three sacraments imprint a character, namely, Baptism, Confirmation, and Order.[85]

The character imprinted on the soul of the priest is the power to dispense the sacraments.[86] Since St. Thomas said that in Holy Orders the priest is deputed to act on behalf of the Church, this spiritual power is its principal effect. "Order denotes power (*potestatem*) principally."[87] This power is for acting on behalf of the Church; to ensure the validity of the sacraments, the priest is sealed with a character. Aquinas states that Christ is the source of all priesthood and the priest of the new law acts *in persona Christi*.[88]

Regarding the priestly character, Thomas further explained that the priest not only stands *in persona Christi*, but also *in persona Ecclesiae*.[89]

> In another way on the part of the whole Church, [...] the priest alone exercises acts immediately directed to God; because to impersonate the Church belongs to him alone who consecrates the Eucharist, which is the sacrament of the universal Church.[90]

The sacraments are not produced by the priest as if he were the efficient cause; he is the instrumental cause. It is the priest, by virtue of who he is ontologically, who prays on behalf of the whole Church. He is truly a mediator as he stands *in persona Christi*, just as Christ is the Mediator between God and man. As the priest shares in the Priesthood of Jesus Christ, so too he shares in the mediatorship of the Lord on behalf of the Church; he stands *in persona Ecclesiae*.[91] Therefore, the validity of the sacraments rest on the validity of the ordination and is not because a priest is holy, learned, or charitable.[92] St. Thomas uses the analogy of a pipe through which water flows. The pipe may be made of silver or lead, yet the water still flows through this instrument. "Therefore the ministers of the Church can confer the sacraments though they be wicked."[93]

St. Thomas' teaching in the *Summa Theologiae* regarding the sacramental character being impressed in the soul of the priest is clear. This character is a spiritual power which deputes the minister to make present the mysteries of Christ in Christian worship.[94] The character configures the priest to Christ, the High Priest. The sacramental character of Holy Orders makes the priest's sacramental ministry a gift to the Church. It ensures the validity of the sacraments conferred. To the priest, it is a reminder of his permanent relationship with Christ, the High Priest. The character provides the priest with the power to fulfill that which is expected of him by the Church. Knowledge of the theology of the character also serves as a reminder to the priest that the dispensation of the sacraments does not depend upon his worthiness; the mark is indelible and cannot be effaced even by his sinfulness. However, this does not relieve the priest of leading a life of holiness; rather it should intensify it. This brief Thomistic section sets the tone for the Church's subsequent teachings regarding the sacramental character.

Magisterial Development

From 1414 to 1418, the Council of Constance was held, in part, to condemn the works of John Wycliffe in Britain and John Hus in Bohemia. Wycliffe and Hus were forerunners of the Protestant reformation. During Session Eight (May 4, 1415), the forty-five articles of John Wycliffe were condemned. The fourth article demonstrated his faulty sacramental theology of Holy Orders: "If a bishop or priest is in mortal sin, he does not ordain or confect or baptize."[95] By condemning this article, the council was not excusing or encouraging sin but rather upholding the validity of the sacraments, regardless of the disposition of the priest.

The Council of Florence (1431 to 1445), the seventeenth ecumenical council, is truly a precursor to the theological teachings of the Council of Trent. This Council tried once more to reconcile and achieve reunion with the Greeks, Armenians, and Jacobites. In the Decree for the Armenians (*Bulla unionis Armenorum* on November 22, 1439), the use of the word *character* is seen in a conciliar document for the first time: "Three of the sacraments, namely baptism, confirmation and orders, imprint indelibly on the soul a character, that is a kind of a stamp which distinguishes it from the rest. Hence they are not repeated in the same person. The other four, however, do not imprint a character and can be repeated."[96]

Council of Trent

The Council of Trent (1545 to 1563), the Church's official response to the Protestant Reformation, produced the longest and most theological treatise on the priesthood of any council. This Council dedicated four chapters and eight canons to the reform of the clergy.[97] During the Seventh Session (March 3, 1547), the Fathers of Trent stated that the three sacraments of Baptism, Confirmation, and Holy Orders all imprint "a character, namely a spiritual and indelible mark" upon the soul.[98] The teachings of Trent simply "expressed what the church had believed and practiced in the course of her history since the beginning."[99]

To understand the teachings of the Council of Trent, it may be helpful to review the perspective of the reformers. Luther, Calvin, and Zwingli all fundamentally denied the reality of the Mass. The Catholic doctrines of Transubstantiation and the Mass as a propitiatory sacrifice, efficacious even for those not present, were their primary objections. Once these doctrines were denied, the priesthood was fundamentally denied. If the Mass is stripped of its meaning, so too is the need for the ministerial priesthood. The understanding of the character disappeared when the effect of the character was no longer needed.[100] In 1520 Martin Luther published *Babylonian Captivity*, also known as the *Pagan Servitude of the Church*, attacking many teachings of the Catholic Church. In the section regarding ordination, Luther wrote:

> I quite fail to see the reason why a man, who has once become a priest, cannot again become a layman, since he only differs from the laity by his ministry. Further, it has not hitherto been impossible for him to be deposed from the ministry, seeing that this punishment is actually imposed from time to time on priests found in fault; they may either be suspended temporarily, or deprived permanently of office. The fiction of the "indelible character" has long been ridiculous.[101]

The Bishops at Trent presented the teachings practiced by Christians from the time of the Apostles. The first chapter of the Twenty-third Session was a compendium of much that had previously been taught by the Church regarding Holy Orders, as well as a defense against the errors of the day. Leaving no room for ambiguity or confusion, the bishops at Trent stressed the sacramental character, this time in the most explicit and detailed manner to date. The fourth chapter of the Twenty-third Session affirmed prior Church teaching regarding Holy Orders:

In the sacrament of order, as in baptism and confirmation, a character is imprinted, which cannot be deleted or removed. Hence the holy synod justifiably condemns the opinion of those who assert that priests of the new covenant have only temporary power, and when duly ordained can be made laity once more if they do not exercise the ministry of the word of God. And if anyone maintains that all Christians without distinction are priests of the new covenant, or that all are equally endowed with the same spiritual power, he appears to be openly overthrowing the church's hierarchy, which is *drawn up as a battle line* (Sg. 6:3 and 9), just as if (against the teaching of blessed Paul, cf. 1 Cor. 12:28-29; Eph. 4:11) all were apostles, all prophets, all evangelists, all pastors, all teachers.[102]

There are several essential points to highlight in the citation above. First of all, it affirms that a character is imprinted on the soul of the priest at ordination. Also, it condemns the view that all Christians, "without distinction," are priests of the new covenant. This does not deny that all Christians are a priestly people (cf. 1 Pt. 2:9), but there is an essential difference when we speak of the ordained priesthood and the priesthood of the laity. The indelibility and permanence of the Sacrament of Holy Orders are affirmed dogmatically by Trent. "Protestants laid such stress upon the universal priesthood of the faithful that they ended up denying that there is any distinction in essence between a layman and an ordained priest."[103] Hence the Tridentine Fathers felt the need to proclaim the longest, most systematic teaching on the priesthood of its day.

Post-Tridentine Period

In 1794 Pope Pius VI wrote *Auctorem fidei*, also known as the *Errors of the Synod of Pistoia*, to correct errors of that Jansenist synod; a number of these errors pertained to Holy Orders. Pius VI condemned "the doctrine which intimates that there was no other title for ordinations than appointment to some special ministry."[104] The Synod in Pistoia had falsely proposed that an ordained priesthood was not necessary, and any baptized person could fulfill this "ministry." The Jansenists in Pistoia suggested that nothing special was bestowed upon the ordinand setting him apart for sacred worship, thus denying the sacramental character. Pius VI, therefore, affirmed the importance of the ministerial priesthood and the unique role it has within the Church. He affirmed that it is through the ordination of the priest by a bishop that the sacred office is passed on, and that this succession is from the apostolic age. Just over one hundred years later, Pope Leo XIII in 1896, likewise affirmed the necessity of apostolic succession.[105]

Pope Pius XI, in the Encyclical Letter *Ad Catholici Sacerdotii* (1935), reaffirmed the permanent character of the priesthood.

> These august powers are conferred upon the priest in a special Sacrament designed to this end: they are not merely passing or temporary in the priest, but are stable and perpetual, united as they are with the indelible character imprinted on his soul whereby he becomes "a priest forever;" whereby he becomes like

unto Him in whose eternal priesthood he has been made a sharer. Even the most lamentable downfall, which, through human frailty, is possible to a priest, can never blot out from his soul the priestly character.[106]

Pius XI, using the language of ontology, affirmed that ordination imprints on the soul a permanent and indelible character. He also reiterated that the sacraments are not contingent on the priest's worthiness. Nonetheless, the priest is called to lead a holy life and respond to God's grace working in his life. Following this teaching on character, Pope Pius XI wrote:

> But along with this character and these powers, the priest through the Sacrament of Orders receives new and special grace with special helps. Thereby, if only he will loyally further, by his free and personal cooperation, the divinely powerful action of the grace itself, he will be able worthily to fulfill all the duties, however arduous, of his lofty calling. He will not be overborne, but will be able to bear the tremendous responsibilities inherent to his priestly duty [...].[107]

In 1947, Pope Pius XII wrote the Encyclical Letter, *Mediator Dei*, regarding the sacred liturgy. In this work, Pius XII desired to strengthen the understanding of the liturgy and the distinct roles of the priest and the laity. While emphasizing the dignity of all of the baptized, Pius XII wanted also to clearly explain the difference between the priesthood of all of the baptized and the ministerial priesthood.

[Priestly ordination] not only imparts the grace appropriate to the clerical function and state of life, but imparts an indelible "character" besides, indicating the sacred ministers' conformity to Jesus Christ the Priest and qualifying them to perform those official acts of religion by which men are sanctified and God is duly glorified in keeping with the divine laws and regulations. [...] In the same way, actually, that baptism is the distinctive mark of all Christians, and serves to differentiate them from those who have not been cleansed in this purifying stream and consequently are not members of Christ, the sacrament of holy orders sets the priest apart from the rest of the faithful who have not received this consecration. For they alone, in answer to an inward supernatural call, have entered the august ministry, where they are assigned to service in the sanctuary and become, as it were, the instruments God uses to communicate supernatural life from on high to the Mystical Body of Jesus Christ. Add to this, as We have noted above, the fact that they alone have been marked with the indelible sign "conforming" them to Christ the Priest, and that their hands alone have been consecrated "in order that whatever they bless may be blessed, whatever they consecrate may become sacred and holy, in the name of our Lord Jesus Christ."[108]

The Magisterial teachings of the Church have confirmed the Tradition of the Scriptures and the early Church Fathers. The theology of the sacramental character was explicitly explained as the Church came to a clearer understanding of what had always been implicit. When certain doctrines of the faith come into question, the Church responds by clarifying, and at times even defining, certain teachings. Such a development has occurred in the case of character. This teaching on the character protects the Church from depending radically on the subjective holiness of the priest and ensures the validity of the sacraments. God's grace is thus freely given to His people through the sacraments of the Church. It is Christ the High Priest Who is operating through the instrumentality of the priest.

Second Vatican Council

A common fallacy today is to believe that Vatican Council II (1962-1965) said nothing about the priesthood, and hence confusion followed. However, the contrary is true; several documents the Second Vatican Council reaffirmed the sacramental character of the ministerial priesthood and the priest's unique role within the Church. One commentator writes:

> The Council of Trent used the concepts of sacramental "character" and supernatural "priestly power," to describe theological being, that is to say, the supernatural being of the priest as constituted by grace. Vatican II continued to build on these bases. The doctrine of the "special character" of the ministerial priesthood is repeated and completed when

the Council affirms that priests are marked with a special character and are so configured (*configurantur*) to Christ the Priest (*Christo Sacerdoti*) that they act in the person of Christ the Head (*PO* 2).[109]

At the end of the Second Vatican Council, on December 7, 1965, *Presbyterorum Ordinis*, the "Decree on the Ministry and Life of Priests," was issued. Regarding the mission of the priesthood, the decree states:

As it is joined to the episcopal order, the priesthood shares in the authority with which Christ himself constitutes, sanctifies and rules his body. Hence the priesthood of the presbyteral order presupposes the sacraments of Christian initiation, but is conferred by the particular sacrament in which priests are sealed with a special mark (*speciali charactere signantur*) by the anointing of the Holy Spirit, and thus are patterned (*configurantur*) to the priesthood of Christ, so that they may be able to act in the person of Christ, the head of the body (*in persona Christi capitis*). [...] Through the ministry of priests the spiritual self-offering of the faithful is celebrated in union with the sacrifice of Christ, the one mediator, in that by their hands it is offered in the name of the whole Church in a sacramental and unbloody manner the eucharist, until the Lord himself shall come (*PO* 2).

Reaffirmed by the Council, and of ultimate importance for this book, is the declaration that the priest is "sealed with a special mark (*charactere*)."[110] Vatican II acknowledged that the sacramental character of the priesthood seals him and "configures" him to the priesthood of Christ. "The essence of the priesthood is a 'configuration' to Christ; *in persona Christi* often occurs in the conciliar texts."[111] The Conciliar Fathers chose not to use the term *alter Christus,* choosing rather *in persona Christi* in order to better elucidate and expand their understanding of the priesthood.[112] While every Christian can be understood to be *alter Christus,* the phrase *in persona Christi* has a particular significance in reference to the ministerial priest. This term carries with it a stronger sense of representation or presence.[113] This teaching was then expounded upon by the Council Fathers. *Presbyterorum Ordinis* built on what had already been stated in the previous conciliar documents regarding the priest being configured and acting in the person of Christ (cf. *SC* 33, *LG* 10, 21, and 28). Lest the phrase *in persona Christi* be left open to misunderstanding, a nuance was introduced by the addition of the word *capitis* (*PO* 2).[114] There is evidence of "genuine doctrinal development on this point."[115] The addition of *capitis* emphasizes that every baptized person is a member of the Body of Christ, but in a particular way, it is the priest who represents Christ, the Head of the Body (cf. Eph. 1:23).[116] Vatican II clearly affirmed the Church's teaching regarding the sacramental character: the priest has been "sealed with a special mark" and is thus configured to Christ the Head.

One of the Conciliar Fathers requested that presbyters be referred to primarily as "ministers of the Church." This was rejected because, as the *Relatio* states: "Presbyters act not as ministers of the Church, but as ministers of Christ."[117] The ministry of the priest proceeds directly from Christ; only secondarily does the priest speak in the name of the Church (or in the person of the Church). The commission responded with the addition of *nomine totius ecclesiae* to *Presbyterorum Ordinis* 2.[118] The strong emphasis on the priest acting in the person of Christ points to the Second Vatican Council's true desire to emphasize the ontological distinctiveness of the ministerial priesthood.[119]

Regarding what has already been stated in *Presbyterorum Ordinis* and *Lumen Gentium*, it is important to remember that there is only one priesthood, that of Christ, the High Priest. Both the baptized and the ordained share in the one and same priesthood of Christ but in ways that render them different "in essence and not only in degree" (*LG* 10).[120] *Lumen Gentium* 10 is the most important conciliar text regarding the distinction between the laity and the ordained. Cardinal Avery Dulles, S.J., commented on the nuance or rediscovery in *Lumen Gentium* 10 regarding the two priesthoods:

> Vatican II made an attempt to rethink the Catholic teaching from a standpoint that was at once more biblical, more ecumenical, and more contemporary. Without discarding the traditional concept of ministerial priesthood, it reworked that concept in light of the New Testament, partly, no doubt, in the hope of achieving a rapprochement with Protestantism. In doing so the council revived the concept of the common priesthood of the whole people of God, which had been practically dormant in Catholic theology. It depicted the ministerial priesthood as oriented in service toward the common priesthood of the baptized.[121]

The Fathers of Vatican II attempted to make the distinction and show the importance of both, without denigrating the importance of either. If the ministerial priesthood alone is stressed, then the value of the common priesthood is overlooked. If the priesthood of the faithful is uniquely highlighted, then confusion ensues regarding the importance of the ministerial priesthood. This balance was not maintained in the years following the Council.

The ministerial priest is able to stand in the person of Christ because he has been essentially configured to the High Priest and ordered to offer His sacrifice. Both priesthoods are *from* and *of* Christ the High Priest but are, nonetheless, ordered to different missions in the Church, while remaining interrelated. The ministerial priesthood is at the service of the common priesthood. The ordained are thus at the service of all of the baptized. Cardinal Dulles wrote:

> It obviously does not mean that the ordained priest undergoes an essential change, thereby ceasing to be a partaker in our common humanity. The distinction is not between two kinds of person but two kinds of priesthood. The council refuses to attribute a higher grade or degree to the ministerial, as though the common priesthood ranked lower than it on the same scale. Instead, it situated the two kinds of priesthood in different categories, like oranges and apples. [...] If anything, the common priesthood is more exalted, for the ministers are ordained for the sake of service toward the whole people of God.[122]

The ministerial priesthood is Christ's own choice for authentically ensuring His sacramental presence to His people. Vatican II emphasized that as the power and teaching authority of Christ flowed "from his very being," so too does the power of Christ flow through his priestly representatives.[123] This power flows from the fact of their ontological change since they have been configured to Christ the High Priest.

By virtue of the sacramental character, the priestly authority of Christ is given to the ordained to sanctify, teach, and govern (*LG* 21 and 28; *PO* 2). This threefold office, or *triplex munus*, finds its origin in the ministry of Christ, Who is *the* Priest, Prophet, and King. Donald Goergen, O.P., noted: "The Second Vatican Council used this threefold typology for understanding episcopal, presbyteral, and diaconal ministry as well as the ministry of all of the baptized (*Lumen Gentium* 10-13, 20-21, 25-31, 34-36)."[124] From the moment of their ordination, priests share in the *tria munera* of Christ in order to teach and preach (*munus docendi* or *propheticum*), sanctify through the sacraments (*munus sanctificandi*), and govern or pastor (*munus regendi*) the people of God (*PO* 4-6 respectively).

The Council reminded the Church of the permanent character of the priesthood, as well as emphasizing the call of her priests to embrace lives of holiness.

> [T]hough the grace of God can achieve the work of salvation even through unworthy ministers, yet in the ordinary way of things God prefers to manifest his wonders through those who have become highly sensitive to the movement and guidance of the Holy Spirit, and because of their close union with Christ

and holiness of life are able to say with the apostle: "It is no longer I who live, but Christ who lives in me" [Gal. 2:20] (*PO* 12).

The sacerdotal character provides the priest the power to do that which he is called to do. He is to perform his priestly functions and respond to his unique call to holiness; in fact, the character is a dynamism for priestly holiness. The vision of the Council was that there must be an integration of life, ministry, and prayer within the priest.

1971 Synod of Bishops

Already by the 1971 Synod of Bishops, many defections from the active ministry had taken place. Immediately following the Council there was great confusion in the Church and in the world regarding the truth and permanence of the priesthood. One author commented:

> The post-conciliar period has been marked by a great deal of turmoil in regard to the ministerial priesthood. By the late 1960s in many countries it already seemed to be in a state of crisis. Vocations dropped, some priests left the active ministry, while many others underwent what at the time was referred to as an identity crisis, a profound self-questioning involving both personal and theological elements.[125]

In 1971, the bishops meeting in Rome with Pope Paul VI issued a document entitled *Ultimis Temporibus: The Ministerial Priesthood and Justice in the World*. In the

Introduction to this document, they revealed the exact nature of their concerns in the post-Vatican II period.

> Happily, the recent Council has recalled the traditional and fruitful teaching on the common priesthood of the faithful. But from this, as by a swing of the pendulum, certain questions have arisen which seem to obscure the position of the priestly ministry in the Church and which deeply trouble the minds of some priests and faithful (*UT* Intro., 4).

This "swing of the pendulum" happened in a very short period of time and left many of the faithful asking questions regarding the essence of the ministerial priesthood. The bishops thus continue by reviewing the questions of the day:

> Does the priestly ministry have any specific nature? Is this ministry necessary? Is it true that the priesthood, of its very nature, cannot be lost? What does being a priest mean today? Would not Christian communities be sufficiently served by presidents designated for the preservation of the common good, without sacramental ordination, and exercising their office for a fixed period? (*UT* Intro., 4).

These "questions of the day" strike the core of the ministerial priesthood; therefore, the bishops desired to reaffirm the indelible character of the priesthood. Even in the naming of the document, the stress is on "ministerial priesthood," not on priestly ministry. The title itself offers a reflection on the ontological character of the priesthood, which is first about being and then about doing.[126] The 1971

Synod simply restated the teachings of the Second Vatican Council, which had concluded only six years prior.

> Among the various charisms and services, only the priestly ministry of the New Testament – which continues Christ's function as mediator, and which is distinct in essence and not merely in degree from the common priesthood of the faithful – perpetuates the essential work of the Apostles [...] (*UT* I, 4).

Lumen Gentium 10 is explicitly cited, restating the distinctiveness of the ontological character of the ministerial priesthood. The bishops state: "Only a priest is able to act in the person of Christ in presiding over and effecting the sacrificial banquet wherein the People of God are associated with Christ's offering (cf. *LG* 28)" (*UT* I, 4). The Synodal Fathers remind the Church that the priest alone stands *in persona Christi* at the altar of the Lord.

The bishops continue by presenting the Church's teaching regarding the permanence of the priestly office grounded in the sacramental character of Holy Orders. Reviewing the history of Orders, they write:

> By the laying on of hands there is communicated a gift of the Holy Spirit which cannot be lost (cf. 2 Tim. 1:6). This reality configures the ordained minister to Christ the Priest, consecrates him (cf. *PO* 2) and makes him a sharer in Christ's mission under its two aspects of authority and service (*UT* I, 5).

They are placing the teaching regarding Holy Orders in historical continuity with the Scriptures and underscoring the permanence of the ministry. Continuing with the theme of permanence, they emphatically state:

> The lifelong permanence of this reality which imprints a sign – and this is a doctrine of faith referred to in Church tradition as the priestly character – expresses the fact that Christ irrevocably associated the Church with himself for the salvation of the world [...]. The minister, whose life bears the seal of the gift received through the Sacrament of Orders, reminds the Church that God's gift is irrevocable (*UT* I, 5).

If there was any doubt as to the Church's teaching regarding the sacramental character, the bishops' response was "strong and clear" that "this is a doctrine of the faith."[127] The Synod of 1971 confronted the issues facing the Church in a definitive and rather decisive way.[128]

Reflecting on the 1971 Synod of Bishops, one of its theological secretaries and drafters, Fr. Hans Urs von Balthasar wrote:

> Its most important accomplishment in this regard was a theological definition of the indelible "seal" imprinted by priestly ordination. [...] Standing thus with his whole existence at the precise point where these two irrevocables meet, the priest symbolizes both of them – a fact that again underscores his specific obligation to advance from *Sein* [objective ministry] to *Sollen* [subjective commitment] and action.[129]

This document serves to remind priests that they share in the very power and authority of Christ because of the priestly character.[130] "This authority does not belong to the minister as his own: it is a manifestation of the Lord's *exousia*, or power, by which the priest is an ambassador of Christ in the eschatological work of reconciliation (cf. 2 Cor. 5:18-20)" (*UT* I, 5). These are profound words to a Church, which was floundering in the post-conciliar period.

Pope John Paul II

The Church owes a great debt of gratitude to the pontificate of John Paul II (1978-2005), especially for the clear vision of priestly life and ministry he offered to the Church. Beginning the first moments after his election, Pope John Paul II reinforced and highlighted the teaching on the sacerdotal character. In his first "Holy Thursday Letter to Priests" in 1979, he reminded his brother priests:

> *The priesthood in which we share through the sacrament of Orders*, which has been forever "imprinted" on our souls through a special sign from God, that is to say the "character," *remains in explicit relationship with the common priesthood of the faithful*, that is to say the priesthood of all baptized, but at the same time it differs from that priesthood "essentially and not only in degree [*LG* 10]."[131]

John Paul II not only clarified the sacramental character of the priesthood, but he reminded his brothers that it is ordered to the service of the faithful. He wrote of the character as the very "basis of our identity."[132]

The renewal of the presbyterate after Vatican II was one of the major concerns of Pope John Paul II: "A concern for priests and their identity and mission has been a central feature of the papacy under Pope John Paul II. He has touched on the theme of the ministerial priesthood on literally hundreds of occasions, including the talks given to groups of priests in the course of his trips and in his Holy Thursday letters."[133]

Following the 1990 Synod of Bishops, he released the Post-Synodal Apostolic Exhortation *Pastores Dabo Vobis*. John Paul II wrote: "Knowledge of the nature and mission of the ministerial priesthood is an essential presupposition, and at the same time the surest guide and incentive toward the development of pastoral activities in the Church for fostering and discerning vocations to the priesthood and training those called to the ordained ministry" (*PDV* 11). Mature knowledge of who one is and an objective knowledge of the priesthood was an issue of extreme importance in the mind of the late Holy Father. One theologian noted:

> The *truth* about the priest is the object of what we may call *priestly self-knowledge*. This has to do with the knowledge of the priest *of* and *about* himself, something which, we believe, is what John Paul II tries to inculcate in the minds of priests. His overriding concern is for priests to have a crystal clear knowledge of who they are, what they are meant to do, and the reason why they should do it. A dubious perception of oneself as a priest leads to a

dubious exercise of priestly ministry. In the course of time, it inevitably leads the priest to doubt his very existence [or ontological being]. He starts to lose meaning in what he does – a meaning which can only be derived from the strength of his conviction about his priestly identity, based on the correct perception of himself as God's minister.[134]

Knowledge is important if the priest is to be who he is called to be. As the John Paul II stated in *Pastores Dabo Vobis*:

A correct and in-depth awareness of the nature and mission of the ministerial priesthood is the path which must be taken – and in fact the Synod did take it – in order to emerge from the crisis *of priestly identity*. In the Final Address of the Synod I stated: "This crisis arose in the years immediately following the Council. It was based on an erroneous understanding of – and sometimes even a conscious bias against – the doctrine of the Conciliar Magisterium. Undoubtedly, herein lies one of the reasons for the great defections experienced then by the Church, losses which did serious harm to pastoral ministry and priestly vocations, especially missionary vocations. It is as though the 1990 Synod, rediscovering by means of many statements which we heard in this hall, the full depth of priestly identity, has striven to instill hope in the wake of these sad losses. These statements showed an awareness of the specific ontological bond which unites the priesthood to Christ the High Priest and Good Shepherd. This identity is built

> upon the type of formation which must be provided for priesthood and then endure throughout the priest's whole life. This was the precise purpose of the Synod (*PDV* 11).

The Pope spoke of a "crisis of priestly identity" resulting from "erroneous understanding." The crisis, in part, is rooted in a lack of knowledge or denial of the truth of Christ's teaching regarding the dignity of the priesthood.

Pope John Paul II reiterated the importance of the sacramental character again during the Jubilee of the Year 2000. He wrote in his "Holy Thursday Letter" that even in the darkness of the *mysterium iniquitatis*, the priesthood of Jesus Christ shines through.[135]

> In all of you I honor the image of Christ you received at your consecration, the "character" that marks each of you indelibly. It is a sign of the special love every priest has come to know and upon which he can always rely, either to move ahead joyfully or to make a fresh start with renewed enthusiasm, in the hope of ever greater fidelity.[136]

Fidelity to the priestly calling leads the priest to a more joy-filled expression of his life. The priest has received a radical and unique call from Love Himself to love others. The Pope continued: "The sacramental character that distinguishes them by virtue of their reception of Holy Orders ensures that their presence and ministry are unique, indispensable and irreplaceable."[137] He affirmed his priests by reminding them that their presence is essential for the life of the Church.[138]

In the year 2003, he wrote his fourteenth and final Encyclical Letter, *Ecclesia de Eucharistia*, on the Eucharist in Its relationship to the Church. He wrote:

> The expression repeatedly employed by the Second Vatican Council, according to which "the ministerial priest, acting in the person of Christ, brings about the Eucharistic Sacrifice" [*LG* 10], was already firmly rooted on papal teaching. As I have already pointed out on other occasions, the phrase *in persona Christi* "means more than offering 'in the name of' or 'in the place of' Christ. *In persona* means in specific sacramental identification with the eternal High Priest who is the author and principal subject of this sacrifice of his, a sacrifice which, in truth, nobody can take his place" [*Dominicae Cenae*, 8]. The ministry of priests who have received the sacrament of Holy Orders, in order of the economy of salvation chosen by Christ, makes clear that the Eucharist which they celebrate is a *gift which radically transcends the power of the assembly* and is in any event essential for validly linking the Eucharistic consecration to the sacrifice of the Cross and to the Last Supper.[139]

Even in his twenty-fifth year as Supreme Pontiff, he did not tire of presenting the sacramental nature and identity of the priest as a unique ministry and gift to the Church.

Pope Benedict XVI

Pope Benedict XVI has sustained the same strong emphasis that his predecessor did concerning the unique nature of the priesthood in the life of the Church. Elected in 2005, he has used opportunities to speak formally (*Ad Limina* addresses) and informally (question and answer sessions with priests) on the gift of the priesthood. Speaking to a group of priests in Warsaw, he said:

> Believe in the power of your priesthood! By virtue of the sacrament, you have received all that you are. When you utter the words "I" and "my" ("I absolve you ... This is my body ..."), you do it not in your own name, but in the name of Christ, "*in persona Christi,*" who wants to use your lips and your hands, your spirit of sacrifice and your talent.[140]

Pope Benedict has confirmed the teaching of the priest standing *in persona Christi*, and at the same time, he has challenged those same men to a radical servitude because of the gift they have received. As Cardinal Ratzinger, he wrote:

> The concept of "servant" is connected with the image of the "indelible character" that belongs to the heritage of faith of the Church. In the language of late antiquity, the word *character* designed the brand that was impressed on a person's property, an object, an animal or even a person, in a way that could never be canceled. The property is identified in an irrevocable way and the legal principle *clamat ad Dominum*

(calls for its owner) comes into play. One could say: "character" means ownership impressed upon the essence.[141]

The vocation to follow and serve Christ as a priest is a mystery the priest is called to embrace as a gift and respond to with loving fidelity. In 2006, as pope, he emphasized:

> The mystery of our priesthood consists in that identification with Him by virtue of which we, poor and weak human beings, through the Sacrament of Orders can speak and act *in persona Christi capitis.* The whole journey of our life and behaviour, with the gift and mystery we have received.[142]

Sacred Scripture, Sacred Tradition, and the Magisterium of the Church all illuminate the reality of the sacramental character of the priesthood. Retaining its original potency, the theological understanding of priesthood has developed and deepened since the days of the Apostles. Yet in certain arenas, this teaching was and is not believed or embraced, particularly in this post-conciliar time. What happened after Vatican II to cause so much confusion regarding something so clearly and consistently taught by the Church?[143]

Notes

1 *Our Priest is Christ* (Roma: P. I. B., 1977), 3. Fr. Vanhoye was elevated to the College of Cardinals on March 24, 2006 by Pope Benedict XVI.

2 "Eucharist, Communion and Solidarity," *ORE*, 13 Nov. 2002, 6.

3 *ST* II-II, q. 166, a. 1, *ad* 1.

4 Fr. Baker explains this reality, "Because of the permanent character received in ordination, they remain priests forever but, if they are legitimately 'laicized' by Church authority, they are dispensed from the obligations of the priesthood (particularly celibacy and the requirement to pray the Divine Office each day) and are forbidden to function as a priest in preaching and administering the sacraments. But even a laicized priest can hear the confession of someone who is dying [...]" (Kenneth Baker, S.J., *Fundamentals of Catholicism,* vol. 3 [San Francisco: Ignatius Press, 1983, reprint, 1985], 326). The administration of the sacraments by a laicized priest is only to be done in what the *Code of Canon Law* refers to as *"in periculo mortis"* (cf. *CIC* 976 and 290).

5 "[...] Scripture is normative for the interior form of the revelation which expresses itself in it. The Church's pneumatic eye is able to read this form in the Scripture, and to this extent, the *pneuma* of Scripture is the *norma normans* for the entire form of ecclesial dogmatics" (Hans Urs von Balthasar, *The Glory of the Lord: A Theological Aesthetics,* vol. 1, *Seeing the Form,* trans. Erasmo Leiva-Merikakis [San Francisco: Ignatius Press, 1982], 591; cf. also, 522-593).

6 Jean Galot, *Theology of the Priesthood,* trans. Roger Balducelli (San Francisco: Ignatius Press, 1985), 87.

7 Cf. International Theological Commission, *From the Diakonia of Christ to the Diakonia of the Apostles: Historico-Theological Research Document* (London: CTS, 2003), 4, 8-10; Galot, *The Theology of the Priesthood,* 160-164; Patrick J. Dunn, *Priesthood: A Re-examination of the Roman Catholic Theology of the Presbyterate* (New York: Alba House, 1990), 50-52; Aidan Nichols, O.P., *Holy Order: Apostolic Priesthood from the New Testament to the Second Vatican Council* (Dublin: Veritas Publications, 1990), 18-20.

8 "Brothers, select from among you seven reputable men, filled with the Spirit and wisdom, whom we shall appoint to this office" (Acts 6:3).

9 Cf. Raymond E. Brown S.S., *Priest and Bishop: Biblical Reflections* (Mahwah, New Jersey: Paulist Press, 1970), 65-73. Raymond Brown discusses the differences, similarities, and development of these two early titles: πρεσβύτεροι (priests/presbyters) and ἐπισκόποι (bishops/overseers). Although the Sacrament of Holy Orders contains three distinct degrees or

orders, the office of deacon will not be discussed in the scope of this paper, since we are primarily concerned with the character of the priestly orders of the presbyterate and the episcopate. (For a further discussion on this topic see the 2003 document of the International Theological Commission, 75-77.) Fr. Quasten, in his commentary on the *Didache* (ca. 100-150 A.D.), says the distinction is not clear from this earliest source of Church doctrine: "The heads of the communities are called *episcopoi* and *diakonoi*; but whether these *episcopoi* were simple priests or bishops is not clear" (cf. Johannes Quasten, *Patrology*, vol. 1, *The Beginnings of Patristic Literature* [Utrecht, Holland: Spectrum, 1950; reprint, Westminster, Maryland: Christian Classics, Inc., 1993], 33).

10 Cf. Acts 6:6; 2 Tim. 1:6; 1 Tim. 4:14; 1 Tim. 5:17-22; Acts 14:23. Cf. also, *Konkordanz Zum Novum Testamentum Graece* (Berlin: Walter de Gruyter, 1987), 674-675.

11 Outside the Acts of the Apostles (14:23 and 20:17), the word *presbyter*, in the sense of a community leader, is used in six epistles: 1 Tim. 5:17, 19; Tit. 1:5; James 5:14; 1 Pt. 5:1; 2 Jn. 1; 3 Jn. 1. The text of Tit. 1:5 orders Titus to establish "presbyters" in every city (cf. Albert Vanhoye, *Sacerdotes Antiguos, Sacerdote Nuevo: Segun el Nuevo Testamento*, trans. Alfonso Ortiz [Salamanca: Ediciones Sigueme, 1984], 276, footnote 55).

12 G. Rambaldi, "Christ's Priesthood and the Ministerial Priesthood in the Church," in *Priesthood and Celibacy*, eds. J. Coppens *et al* (Roma: Editrice Àncora, 1972), 403-404.

13 Definitions offered in the *Greek-English Lexicon* help to broaden the scope of the meaning of *sphragis*: "the substance which bears the imprint of a signet and seals a document, *seal* (Rev. 5:1)"; "the impression made by a signet, *mark* (2 Tim. 2:19)" (BDAG 980-981).

14 Cf. 2 Cor. 1:21-22, Eph. 1:13-14 and 4:30. These texts are not referring solely to priesthood, but also to the baptized who have been "marked" or "sealed" by the primary sacrament which also confers an indelible character.

15 *Concordance to the Septuagint*, vol. 2, eds. Edwin Hatch and Henry Redpatch (Graz, Austria: Akademische Druck, 1954), 1454.

16 *Brown-Driver-Briggs Hebrew and English Lexicon* (Peabody, MA.: Hendrickson, 2000), 863.

17 Patrick J. Dunn, *Priesthood: A Re-examination of the Roman Catholic Theology of the Presbyterate*, 142 (cf. 142-144 for a succinct synopsis of "*sphragis*" in the Scriptures and in the Fathers).

18 Cf. John Macquarrie, *A Guide to the Sacraments* (London: SCM Press, 1997), 185. The *Greek-English Lexicon* offers four definitions: "a mark or impression placed on an object – of coinage *impress, reproduction,*

representation – or of a distinguishing mark *trademark*"; "something produced as a representation, *reproduction, representation* (Heb. 1:3)" ; "characteristic trait or manner, *distinctive mark*" ; "an impression that is made, *outward aspect, outward appearance, form*" (BDAG 1077-1078).

19 Private translation.

20 Cf. Macquarrie, *A Guide to the Sacraments*, 184-186.

21 Brown, *Priest and Bishop: Biblical Reflections*, 19-20.

22 Donald W. Wuerl, *The Catholic Priesthood Today* (Chicago: Franciscan Herald Press, 1976), 161. *The Catholic Priesthood Today* is a popularized version of his doctoral dissertation from the *Angelicum* (Rome, 1974), entitled, "The Priesthood: The Doctrine of the Third Synod of Bishops and Recent Theological Conclusions."

23 A. Nichols, *Holy Order*, 33.

24 Irenaeus, *Adversus Haereses* 3, 3, 3: *PG* 7, 849: *EnchP* 211: trans. ANF 1 and *Commentary on St. John* 6, 36: trans. Quasten, 1, 42. This point is made to emphasize the close connectedness of the early Church Fathers with the Apostles and their teaching.

25 Francis A. Sullivan, S.J., *From Apostles to Bishops: The Development of the Episcopacy in the Early Church* (New York: The Newman Press, 2001), 91.

26 Clement of Rome, *Epistula ad Corinthios I*, 44, 1-2: *PG* 1, 296-297: *EnchP* 21: trans. ANF 1.

27 Sullivan, *From Apostles to Bishops: The Development of the Episcopacy in the Early Church*, 96.

28 Kenan B. Osborne, O.F.M., *Priesthood: A History of the Ordained Ministry in the Roman Catholic Church* (Mahwah, New Jersey: Paulist Press, 1988), 94-95.

29 Cf. *Epistula ad Magnesios* 6, 1: *PG* 5, 668: *EnchP* 44: trans. ANF 1.

30 *Epistula ad Smyrnaeos* 8, 2: *PG* 5, 713: *EnchP* 65: trans. ANF 1.

31 Irenaeus, *Adversus haereses* 4, 26, 2: *PG* 7, 1053-1054: *EnchP* 237: ANF 1.

32 Sullivan, *From Apostles to Bishops: The Development of the Episcopacy in the Early Church*, 150-151.

33 *Synthèse Dogmatique: de la Trinité à la Trinité* (Paris: Beauchesne, 1985), 1112.

34 William A. Jurgens, *The Faith of the Early Fathers* (Collegeville: Liturgical Press, 1970), 1, 118.

35 Tertullian, *De praescriptione haereticorum* 41: *PL* 2, 56-57: *EnchP* 300: trans. ANF 3.

36 Hippolytus, *Apostolic Tradition*: *PG* 10, 869: trans. *The Treatise on the*

Apostolic Tradition, eds. Gregory Dix and Henry Chadwick (London: Alban Press, 1992), 1-72.

37   *The Treatise on the Apostolic Tradition*, 13. The Greek word, *cheirotonein*, comes from the word, *cheir*, meaning hand.

38   David N. Power, O.M.I., *Ministers of Christ and His Church: The Theology of the Priesthood* (London: Geoffrey Chapman, 1969), 31. The verse cited above can also be translated, "So now, O Lord , grant that there may be preserved among us unceasingly the Spirit of Thy grace, and make us worthy that in faith we may minister to Thee in singleness of heart praising Thee" (*The Treatise on the Apostolic Tradition*, 14).

39   *The Theology of Ordained Ministry in the Letters of Augustine of Hippo* (San Francisco: International Scholars Publications, 1998), 58-59.

40   "Elements for a Theology of Priesthood in the Teaching of the Fathers of the Church," in *Priests: Identity and Ministry*, ed. Robert J. Wister (Wilmington, Delaware: Michael Glazier, 1990), 32-33.

41   "The Priesthood According to the Magisterium from Lateran IV to the Council of Trent," in *Priesthood and Celibacy*, eds. J. Coppens *et al* (Roma: Editrice Àncora, 1972), 144.

42   "Life and Ministry of Priests," in *Priesthood: A Greater Love – International Symposium on the Thirtieth Anniversary of the Promulgation of the Conciliar Decree Presbyterorum Ordinis*, 28 October 1995, 86-87. Cf. also Gerhard Müller, *Priesthood and Diaconate: The Recipient of the Sacrament of Holy Orders from the Perspective of Creation Theology and Christology*, trans. Michael J. Miller (San Francisco: Ignatius Press, 2002), 193-194.

43   Ibid.

44   Coppens, *Priesthood and Celibacy*, 21.

45   Cf. Hermae Pastor, *Similitudines* 9, 17, 4: *PG* 2, 998: *EnchP* 93: trans. ANF 2; Eusebius Pamphilus, *Historia Ecclesiastica* 6, 5, 6: PG 20, 533: trans. NPNF 2, 1; Ephrem the Syrian, *de Virg. Maria* 4, 9: *CSCO* 224, 26: trans. Auer, 69 (cf. Johann Auer and Joseph Ratzinger, *Dogmatic Theology*, vol. 6, *A General Doctrine of the Sacraments and the Mystery of the Eucharist*, trans. Erasmo Leiva-Merikakis, ed. Hugh M. Riley (Washington, D.C.: CUA Press, 1995), 69.

46   Canon 8: trans. DEC, 9.

47   *The Priest in Union with Christ*, trans. G. W. Shelton (Cork, Ireland: Mercier Press, 1951; reprint, Rockford, Illinois: TAN, 2002), 20.

48   *In Sanctum Baptisma*, *Oratio* 40, 26: *PG* 36, 396: trans. NPNF 2, 7 (preached on 6 January 381).

49   Cf. *In epistulam I ad Corinthios homiliae* 8, 2: *PG* 61, 69: *EnchP* 1189: trans. NPNF 1, 12.

50 Chrysostom, *In Matthaeum homiliae* 50, 3: *PG* 58, 507: trans. NPNF 1, 10. Cf. also *In epistulam II ad Timotheum, homiliae* 2, 4: *PG* 62, 612: *EnchP* 1207: trans. NPNF 1, 13.

51 *De Sacerdotio* 3, 5: *PG* 48, 643: *EnchP* 1119: trans. NPNF 1, 9.

52 Cf. *A Patristic Greek Lexicon*, ed. G. W. H. Lampe, D.D. (Oxford: Clarendon Press, 1961), 980 and BDAG 740.

53 BDAG 642.

54 K. Baker, *Fundamentals of Catholicism*, vol. 3, 179.

55 *De Baptismo, contra Donatistas* 1, 4, 5: *PL* 43, 112: trans. NPNF 1, 4.

56 Jan Michael Joncas, "Ordination, Orders," in *Augustine Through the Ages: An Encyclopedia*, ed. Allan D. Fitzgerald, O.S.A. (Grand Rapids, MI.: William B. Eerdmans, 1999), 601.

57 Kasper, "Ministry in the Church: Taking Issue with Edward Schillebeeckx" in *Communio: International Catholic Review* X, 2 (Summer 1983): 188-189.

58 *Contra Epistolam Parmeniani* 2, 13, 28: *PL* 43, 70 : *EnchP* 1617: trans. Jurgens, 3, 64.

59 Ibid. Cf. also *In Ioannis evangelium tractatus* 5, 18: *PL* 35, 1424: *EnchP* 1810: trans. NPNF 1, 7; *De Baptismo, contra Donatistas* 5, 20, 28: *PL* 43, 190: *EnchP* 1635: trans. NPNF 1, 4.

60 Cf. Emmanuel J. Cutrone, "Sacraments," in *Augustine Through the Ages: An Encyclopedia*, 745.

61 Anastasius II, *Exordium Pontificatus mei*, 7-8: trans. Denz., 169.

62 *Testamentum Domini* (Syriac, Arabic, and Ethiopic versions) as found in Paul F. Bradshaw, *Ordination Rites of the Ancient Churches of East and West* (New York: Pueblo Publishing, 1990), 119.

63 Cf. Armenian (4th c. origins), Bradshaw, 130; Byzantine (8th c. ms.), Bradshaw, 135; Coptic (14th c. ms.), Bradshaw, 147; East Syrian/Chaldean (15th c. ms.), Bradshaw, 161; Georgian (10th c. ms.), Bradshaw, 171; Jacobite (12th c. ms.), Bradshaw, 182; Maronite (13th c. ms.), Bradshaw, 196; Melkite (14th c. ms.), Bradshaw, 210; Roman – Leonine Sacramentary (7th c. ms.), 218; Gallican (5th c. ms.), Bradshaw 227; England – Leofric Missal (10th c. ms.), Bradshaw, 236. Pierre Jounel wrote, "For the ritual of all of the Eastern rites depend more or less directly on the ritual in the *Apostolic Constitutions*; this is true not only in the rites that originated in the patriarchate of Antioch (Western Syrian, Eastern Syrian, Byzantine, Armenian, Maronite), but also of the Coptic rite of the Patriarchate of Alexandria. That is why, despite noteworthy differences, they are fundamentally the same in the number of orders, the rite of ordination, and the sacramental formula itself" ("Ordinations," 147). For

further study of the early rites and prayers of ordination, see James F. Puglisi, S.A., *Epistemological Principles and Roman Catholic Rites*, vol. 1, *The Process of Admission to Ordained Ministry: A Comparative Study* (Collegeville: Liturgical Press, 1996). "The ordination prayers, however, have remained almost identical since the *Sacramentarium Veronense* [Leonine Sacramentary (7th c.)]" (ibid., 190).

64 Other Fathers of the early Church certainly could have been mentioned in this section, such as Origen, Cyprian, Basil, Gregory of Nyssa, Ambrose, Leo the Great, and Gregory the Great (cf. Luigi Padovese, *I Sacerdoti dei Primi Secoli: Testimonianze dei Padri sui Ministri Ordinati* [Roma: Edizioni Collegio S. Lorenzo da Brindisi – Laurentianum, 2002]; Kenan B. Osborne, O.F.M., *Priesthood: A History of the Ordained Ministry in the Roman Catholic Church* [Mahwah, New Jersey: Paulist Press, 1988]). Padovese and Osborne offer a good historical overview of the sacrament of Holy Orders within the early Church.

65 *Oratio in baptismum Christi*: PG 46, 581: *EnchP* 1062: trans. NPNF 2, 5. *Chorizomenon* means "to be separated from" or "different" in a radical way; same word used in Hebrews 2:26 (BDAG 1095).

66 Cf. John Henry Newman, *An Essay on the Development of Christian Doctrine* (1845, reprint, New York: Sheed and Ward, 1960). "Certain doctrines come to us, professing to be Apostolic, and possessed of such antiquity that, though we are only able to assign the date of their formal establishment to the fourth, or the fifth, or the eighth, or the thirteenth c., as it may happen, yet their substance may, for what appears, be coeval with the Apostles, and be expressed or implied in texts of Scripture" (ibid., 73; cf. chap. 3, sec. 1). Cardinal Dulles commented on Newman's importance for the Church today, "In his *Essay on the Development of Christian Doctrine* (1845), Cardinal John Henry Newman gives a full and lengthy defense of change as a sign of vitality in the church. But he insists on what he calls 'preservation of type,' 'continuity of principles' and 'conservative action on the past.' Right from the beginning of his book he excludes the possibility of doctrinal reversals. Those who think that Christianity accommodates itself to times and seasons, he says, usually end up by abandoning the supernatural claims of Christianity – a phenomenon that is no less common today than it was in Newman's day" ("Vatican II: Substantive Teaching," *America*, 31 March 2003, 16).

67 *Decretal Maiores*: *Letter to Humbert, Archbishop of Arles*: trans. ND, 1410 (DS, 781).

68 Galot writes: "The Middle Ages had known a variety of opinions on the nature of sacramental character. From William of Auvergne to St. Thomas and Duns Scotus, theologians had tried to determine with precision the

nature of the sacramental character with or without the help of Aristotelian categories. The character was conceived as a holiness, a capacity-to-be-acted-upon, a disposition, a figure, a sign that signifies grace, a *habitus*, a sign of participation, in the sacraments, a sign of the profession of faith, a relation, a cultic empowerment. Cultic empowerment – St. Thomas' theory – won such great prestige as to be adopted as if no other theory were in sight" (*The Theology of the Priesthood*, 197). Cf. also Ernst Latko, O.F.M., "A Cursory Survey of the Franciscan Contribution to Sacramental Theology," in *Franciscan Approach to Theology: Report on the Thirty-Eighth Annual Meeting of the Franciscan Educational Conference*, Saginaw, Michigan, 20-22 August 1957 (Washington, D.C.: Franciscan Educational Conference, 1958), 199-204.

69 "The mature teaching of St. Thomas with respect to the doctrine of the sacramental character is concentrated in the *Summa Theologica*, III, q. 63. His earlier treatment is found in his *Commentary on the Sentences*, IV, dist. 4" (Richard W. Smith, "Marked with the Sign of Faith: Toward a Contemporary Understanding of the Sacramental Character" [S.T.D. diss., Pontifical Gregorian University (Rome), 1998], 3).

70 *ST* III, q. 63, a.1.

71 *ST* III, q. 63, a.1, *sed contra*.

72 *ST* III, q. 63, a.1, *ad* 2.

73 *ST* III, q. 63, a. 3, *sed contra*.

74 *ST* III, q. 63, a. 3, *responsio*.

75 *ST* III, q. 63, a. 5.

76 *ST* III, q. 63, a. 5, *ad* 2.

77 *ST* III, q. 63, a. 5, *ad* 1.

78 Clement Dillenschneider, C.Ss.R., *Dogmatic Foundations of Our Priestly Spirituality*, vol. 1, *Christ the One Priest and We His Priests* (St. Louis: B. Herder, 1964), 136.

79 Cf. *ST* III, q. 62, a. 5, *ad* 1. "His faithful are likened (*configurentur*) to Him by sharing a certain power (*potestatem*) with regard to the sacraments and to things pertaining to the Divine worship. [...] Now Christ's Priesthood is eternal, according to Ps. cix. 4: *Thou art a priest forever, according to the order of Melchisedech*, consequently, every sanctification wrought by His Priesthood, is perpetual, enduring as long as the thing sanctified endures (*re consecrata manente*)" (*ST* III, q. 62, a. 5).

80 *Ministers of Christ and His Church: The Theology of the Priesthood* (London: Geoffrey Chapman, 1969), 121. Richard Smith wrote, "Though distinct, character and grace are nevertheless recognized as related to each other. This relationship is rooted in the understanding that the character, the *sacramentum et res* of the three sacraments by which it is imprinted, is

the dispositive cause. [...] [T]he profound difference of character and grace, which is not indelible, [is] its [i.e. grace's] presence being dependent on the variable dispositions of the subjects who receive it." Grace can be restored by conversion and penance: *reviviscence* ("Marked with the Sign of Faith: Toward a Contemporary Understanding of the Sacramental Character," 8-9).

81 *ST* III, q. 63, a. 5, *ad* 3.

82 *ST* III, q. 63, a. 1.

83 The Blackfriars commentary to *ST* III, q. 63, a. 1 states, "Earlier commentators were so preoccupied with the aspect of divine cult as the administering and receiving of divine things that they treated of character [*sic*] almost exclusively in terms of the efficient, downward orientated causality of the sacraments. St. Thomas, by contrast, thinks equally of man's activity as directed to God in the cult by faith and charity and the external expression of these through the worship of religion" (vol. 56, 78).

84 *ST* III, q. 63, a. 6 (cf. also *ad* 1).

85 *ST* III, q. 63, a. 6.

86 Cf. *ST* Suppl., q. 34, a. 3.

87 *ST* Suppl., q. 34, a. 2, *ad* 2. And further he wrote, "This sacrament consists chiefly in the power conferred" (*ST* Suppl., q. 34, a. 4).

88 Cf. *ST* III, q. 22, a. 4.

89 cf. *ST* III, q. 64, a. 8, *ad* 2; a. 9, *ad* 1; *ST* Suppl., q. 37, a. 4, *ad* 2.

90 *ST* Suppl., q. 37, a. 4, *ad* 2.

91 Aquinas defines the relationship between these two phrases as follows: "The priest, in reciting the prayers of the mass, speaks instead of the church (*in persona Ecclesiae*), in whose unity he remains; but in consecrating the sacrament he speaks as in the person of Christ (*in persona Christi*), Whose place he holds by the power of his orders. Consequently, if a priest severed from the unity of the Church celebrates mass, not having lost the power of order, he consecrates Christ's true body and blood; but because he is severed from the unity of the Church, his prayers have no efficacy" (*ST* III, q. 82, a. 7, *ad* 3).

92 Timothy McDermott paraphrases the *ST* III, q. 64, a. 1, "So the sacramental effect is no better when administered by a better minister. The minister's devotion may win some associated effect for the recipient, but even that is not something the minister himself produces, but something God produces in response to the minister's prayer" (*St. Thomas Aquinas: Summa Theologiae: A Concise Translation* [Allen, Texas: Christian Classics, 1989], 558).

93 *ST* III, q. 64, a. 5.

94 "Order considered as a sacrament which imprints a character is

specially directed to the sacrament of the Eucharist, in which Christ Himself is contained, because by a character we are made like to Christ Himself" (*ST* Suppl., q. 40, a. 5, *ad* 2).

95   Council of Constance, *Sessio* VIII, *Sententia condemnatoria articulorum Ioannis Wicleff*, 4: trans. DEC 411 and 412.

96   Council of Florence, *Sessio* VIII, *Bulla unionis Armenorum*: trans. DEC 542.

97   Particular teachings on the priesthood are also found in Trent in Chapter 1, Canons 1 and 2 regarding the sacrifice of the Eucharist and its intimate connection to the priesthood, and Canon 9 regarding the sacraments in general.

98   Council of Trent, *Sessio* VII, *Canones de sacramentis in genere*, c. 9: trans. DEC 685.

99   Galot, *The Theology of the Priesthood*, 200.

100   Cf. Diarmaid MacCulloch, *Reformation: Europe's House Divided – 1490-1700* (London: Penguin Books, 2003), 110 and 128-129. Cramner, acting under the influence of Bucer, likewise led the Anglican Communion in its denial of Holy Orders and the Mass during the time of the Reformation. In the *Thirty-Nine Articles* of the Anglican High Church, the 28th and the 31st Articles denied the Real Presence (transubstantiation) and the sacrificial nature of the Mass as "blasphemous fables" (cf. Anthony Stephenson, S.J., *Anglican Orders* [Westminster, Maryland: Newman Press, 1956], 11 and 28 respectively).

101   In *Martin Luther: Selections from his Writings*, ed. John Dillenberger (Garden City, New York: Anchor Books, 1961), 350.

102   Council of Trent, *Sessio* XXIII, *Vera et catholica doctrina de sacramento ordinis ad condemnandos errores nostri temporis*, 4: trans. DEC 742-743 (emphasis in original).

103   Michael Davies, *The Order of Melchisedech: A Defence of the Catholic Priesthood* (Devon, U.K.: Augustine Publishing, 1979), 1.

104   *Auctorem fidei: Errors of the Synod of Pistoia, Ordo*, 5: trans. Denz., 1552.

105   Cf. *Apostolicae Curae: Apostolic Letter on Anglican Ordinations*, 25-26: *ASS* 29, 198. Neuner and Dupuis (499) explain the historical context: "In the Edwardine Ordinal (1552) the rites of ordination of the Roman Pontifical were changed by Cramner acting under the influence of Bucer. The Anglican ordinations performed by the new rite were already considered invalid from the Catholic stand-point by Pope Julius III in a letter to Card. Reginald Pole (1554) and by two letters of Pope Paul IV (Jan. 20 and Oct. 30, 1555). It was concluded that because both the form and the intention were substantially

changed and not of the mind of the Church, the sacramental character was not conferred. *Apostolicae Curae* points to the importance of apostolic succession and proper form in order to confer the sacramental character of Holy Orders."

106 *Ad Catholici Sacerdotii*, 22: *AAS* 28 (1936), 15.

107 Ibid.

108 *Mediator Dei*, 42-43: *AAS* 39 (1947), 539 (Washington, D.C.: USWC, 1948).

109 Paul Hacker, "The Priesthood and the Eucharist Today," in *Priesthood and Celibacy*, eds. J. Coppens *et al* (Roma: Editrice Àncora, 1972), 329.

110 *PO* 2 (cf. also *PO* 6, 12; *OT* 2).

111 Hacker, "The Priesthood and the Eucharist Today," in *Priesthood and Celibacy*, 331. The footnote to this quote cites the phrase *in persona Christi* as being an expression "familiar" to St. Thomas Aquinas: *ST* III, q. 22, a. 4; q. 78, aa. 1 and 4; q. 82, a. 1 (cf. ibid.).

112 Saturnino Gamarra commented on this: "Para todos es conocido que la formulación del sacerdote como 'Alter Christus' se introdujo en el aula conciliar (*ASyn* III, IV, 247; IV, V, 548), y no progresó; pero, encambio, la fórmula 'in persona Christi' aparece desde la primera redacción del esquema del P.O., presentado en noviembre del 1964 (*ASyn* IV, IV, 834). Sólo apuntamos el hecho, indicando que la exclusión del 'Alter Christus' supuso un proceso de profundización" ("El Ministerio Sacerdotal en el Reciente Magisterio de la Iglesia," in *Ministerio Sacerdotal y Trinidad*, vol. 32 [Salamanca: Ediciones Secretariado Trinitario, 1997], 119).

113 Cf. *ASyn* III, VIII, 96-101 (which became *LG* 28).

114 Cf. *ASyn* III, IV, 826, 846; IV, III, 390; IV, IV, 337-338.

115 Sara Butler, "Priestly Identity: 'Sacrament' of Christ the Head" *Worship* 70.4 (July 1996): 293. "The *Acta synodalia* reveal that the council fathers deliberately attempted to clarify still further the nature and theological foundation of the ministerial priesthood and its distinction from the common priesthood in the Decree on the Ministry and Life of Priests" (ibid., 300).

116 The emphasis on the priest and the Church as the Body of Christ is a central theme of *PO* (cf. 1, 6, 8, 9, 12, 15, 22, 25). The primary theme is that of the priest following the example of the Good Shepherd (cf. 3, 5, 6, 9, 11, 13, 14, 18, 22).

117 *ASyn* IV, VII, 123-124.

118 ASyn IV, VII, 110-111, 118-119, 122-123. Preceding *PO* by two years, *SC* 33 makes use both phrases: the priest presiding over the Eucharist *in persona Christi* and the priest praying *in nomine ecclesiae*.

119 In the official "Explanatory Note" (i.e. the appendix) of *Lumen*

Gentium, the actual language of ontology is used: "It is the unmistakable teaching of tradition, including liturgical tradition, that an *ontological* share in the *sacred* functions is given by *consecration* [of bishops]" ("Preliminary Explanatory Note," 2).

120 Cf. F. Ocariz, L. F. Mateo Seco, and J. A. Riestra, *The Mystery of Jesus Christ* (Dublin: Four Corners, 1994), 170-171. "Christ has no successors in his priesthood. Just as he is the only victim, he is the only priest. All other priesthood – the priesthood of the New Covenant – is nothing but a *participation* in this unique priesthood of Jesus Christ, by means of *assimilation* to Christ, *identification* with Christ, *putting on* Christ by means of the sacraments. This happens in the *priesthood of the faithful*, which is conferred in the sacrament of baptism, and in the *ministerial priesthood*, which is received through the sacrament of Order. So, neither the priesthood of the faithful nor the ministerial priesthood follows on from or is added on to Christ's priesthood. They are not successors, because Christ's priesthood is forever, because he continues forever. [...] They are not added to Christ's priesthood, because it is not possible to add either another offering or another victim to the sacrifice which was already made on Calvary. That sacrifice is renewed in the Eucharist, without adding anything essential to what happened at Calvary. It is Christ the Priest himself who, in the Eucharistic celebration, offers himself to the Father through the ministry of priests in an unbloody manner. In this context these words of the Second Vatican Council take on a special force: 'priests by the anointing of the Holy Spirit are signed with a special character and are so configured to Christ the priest in such a way that they are able to act in the person of Christ the head' [*PO* 2]" (ibid., emphasis in the original).

121 *The Priestly Office: A Theological Reflection* (Mahwah, New Jersey: Paulist Press, 1997), 2.

122 Ibid., 11.

123 Cf. *PO* 2, 6, 12; *LG* 19-22, 26-28 (cf. also A. Nichols, *Holy Order: Apostolic Priesthood from the New Testament to the Second Vatican Council*, 133; and Galot, *The Theology of the Priesthood*, 186).

124 "Priest, Prophet, King: The Ministry of Jesus Christ," in *The Theology of the Priesthood*, eds. Donald J. Goergen and Ann Garrido (Collegeville: Liturgical Press, 2000), 191.

125 Daniel Donovan, *What Are They Saying about the Ministerial Priesthood?* (Mahwah, New Jersey: Paulist Press, 1992), 19.

126 Cf. Tommaso Stenico, *Il Presbitero: Vita e Ministero – Sinossi Pastores Dabo Vobis; Presbyterorum Ordinis; Optatam Totius; Ultimis Temporibus; Direttorio per il ministero e la vita dei Presbiteri*, 54.

127 Cf. Gamarra, "El Ministerio Sacerdotal en el Reciente Magisterio de la Iglesia," 133.

128 Cf. ibid., 134.

129 Balthasar, *The Christian State of Life*, trans. Sr. Mary Frances McCarthy (San Francisco: Ignatius Press, 1983), 321. Now bishop, Peter Henrici wrote: "Since its establishment in 1969 to the end of his life, von Balthasar was a member of the International Theological Commission [...]. At the second Synod of Bishops in 1971, on the ministerial priesthood, he worked as one of the theological secretaries and drafted the document on priestly spirituality" ("A Sketch of Von Balthasar's Life," *Hans Urs Von Balthasar: His Life and Work*, ed. David L. Schindler [San Francisco: Ignatius Press, 1991], 35).

130 Cf. Gamarra, 133.

131 John Paul II, "Letter of the Holy Father Pope John Paul II to All Priests of the Church on the Occasion of Holy Thursday 1979," 3 (emphasis in the original), in *Letters to my Brother Priests: Holy Thursday (1979-2001)*. Regarding this letter, Donovan wrote: "In the 1979 letter reference is made to *LG* and *PO* but only *LG* 10 is quoted. [...] The phrase about the two priesthoods differing 'essentially and not only in degree' comes back four times in the 1979 letter. The other phrase, *in persona Christi*, occurs three times in that letter and then periodically throughout the series" (*What Are They Saying about the Ministerial Priesthood?*, 27).

132 Ibid., 4. Dermot Power commented: "For a contemporary spirituality of the ministerial priesthood, a recovery of what is originally meant by the notion of character might lead precisely to the language of gift and grace found in John Paul's letter and to the vision and experience of priestly existence which makes such language possible" (*A Spiritual Theology of the Priesthood: The Mystery of Christ and the Mission of the Priest*), 84.

133 Donovan, *What Are They Saying about the Ministerial Priesthood?*, 25.

134 Peter Mondejar Correa, "The Identity of the Ministerial Priest and his Call to Holiness: A Study in Light of Karol Wojtyla's (John Paul II) Philosophy of the Acting Person," S.T.D. diss. (Pontifical University of St. Thomas Aquinas [Rome], 1989), 98.

135 John Paul II, "Letter of the Holy Father Pope John Paul II to All Priests of the Church on the Occasion of Holy Thursday 2000," 2, in *Letters to my Brother Priests: Holy Thursday (1979-2001)*. This *mysterium iniquitatis* will be mentioned again in the year 2002 in a painful way in light of the priestly sexual misconduct crisis in the United States. "At this time too, as priests we are personally and profoundly afflicted by the sins of some of our brothers who have betrayed the grace of ordination in succumbing even to the

most grievous forms of the *mysterium iniquitatis* at work in the world. Grave scandal is caused, with the result that a dark shadow of suspicion is cast over all the other fine priests who perform their ministry with honesty and integrity and often with heroic self-sacrifice" ("Ministers of Mercy: The Sacrament of Reconciliation – Letter of the Holy Father Pope John Paul II to All Priests of the Church on the Occasion of Holy Thursday 2002," 11, *Origins* 31 [4 April 2002]: 699).

136 "Letter of the Holy Father Pope John Paul II to All Priests of the Church on the Occasion of Holy Thursday 2000," 3.

137 Ibid., 5.

138 Cf. ibid., 10. "Our priesthood was born in the Upper Room together with the Eucharist. [...] In saying 'Do this,' he refers not only to the action, but also to the one who is called to act; in other words, he institutes the ministerial priesthood, which thus becomes one of the essential elements of the Church." Cf. also John Paul II, *Ut Unum Sint: Encyclical Letter on Commitment to Ecumenism* (Vatican City: Libreria Editrice Vaticana, 1995), 50, 59, and 67.

139 *Ecclesia de Eucharistia*, 29.

140 Benedict XVI, "Immerse Yourselves in the Love of the Saviour," *ORE*, 31 May 2006, 2.

141 "Life and Ministry of Priests," in *Priesthood: A Greater Love – International Symposium on the Thirtieth Anniversary of the Promulgation of the Conciliar Decree Presbyterorum Ordinis*, 28 October 1995, 81.

142 "I No Longer Call You Servants, But Friends: To the Italian Bishop's Conference," *ORE*, 24 May 2006, 6.

143 The first chapter of this book has gone to great lengths to emphasize the priestly character in order to show that it is neither a novelty nor obsolete. It is simply the Church's teaching - not the opinion of this author nor of any individual theologian. "Character" may be interpreted philosophically in one way or another as "spiritual power" or "habitus," but the point is that it does exist and it marks the soul permanently, sealing the ordained to the one priesthood of Jesus Christ. For more on these diverse interpretations and on the Second Vatican Council's teaching on the sacerdotal character see Guy Mansini, "Episcopal Munera and the Character of Episcopal Order," *The Thomist* 66 (2002): 369-94 and "Sacerdotal Character at the Second Vatican Council," *The Thomist* 67 (2003): 539-77.

Chapter 2

Post-Conciliar Confusion:
Departing from the Tradition

The first chapter emphasized the Church's teaching on priestly character, which is the foundation of the priestly life. If a priest knows the fullness of the gift received, it will help him live out the gift in its fullness. The gift is given and meant to be a gift for others. The ontological change occurs so that a man can more radically serve the people with a strength that does not ultimately come from him. He acts *in persona Christi*: sacramentally, ministerially, and in fact, at all times. However, many priests educated in the decades following the Second Vatican Council were simply never taught the reality of the sacerdotal character. Some theologians deliberately taught a contradictory doctrine to that of the Church's constant teaching. This chapter will briefly review the difficulties of the day that *Ultimis Temporibus* and *Pastores Dabo Vobis* were seeking to address.

Cultural Upheaval

In the middle of the 1960s a cultural revolution was in its initial stages. This revolution eventually touched every aspect of American society. The transformation of society in this period of time was dramatic – one of the swiftest in recorded history. Things commonplace today were unimaginable before 1965. No single cause is responsible for the present situation. Within the secular world, the combination of the Vietnam War, the sexual revolution, the unrest of the civil rights movement, the dawn of radical feminism, student revolts on American and European campuses, the drug culture, the "hippies," musical and lyrical changes, and the eventual hi-tech phenomena together created a "perfect-storm" for the cultural revolution of the sixties and seventies.

"The good news of the Second Vatican Council (1962-1965) broke out on the world at [this] time of cultural upheaval and revolution."[1] Cardinal Avery Dulles has noted: "The [C]ouncil occurred at a unique moment of history, when the Western world was swept up in a wave of optimism typified by Pope John XXIII himself."[2] On October 11, 1962, Pope John XXIII said: "For with the opening of this Council a new day is dawning on the Church, bathing her in radiant splendor."[3] Little did he know that this would also be the dawning of a very difficult period of history. Msgr. George Kelly observed: "The 1960s was a decade of revolution for which the hierarchy, beginning with the Pope, were ill prepared."[4] The Church "opened its windows just as the modern, western world was barreling into a dark tunnel full of poisonous fumes."[5]

In the midst of the cultural upheaval, the changes of the Second Vatican Council came quickly and without any real thought given to systematic implementation. With the new focus on the common priesthood of all of the faithful, many priests were confused about their place in the Church. Many of the faithful, both clergy and laity, interpreted Vatican II in democratic or egalitarian terms.[6] Ultimately, what was occurring on the societal level, a culture climate of dissent, deeply affected the life of the Church. This period of history was marked by large numbers of priests and religious leaving the active ministry; there was blatant disregard for official Church teaching on faith and morals, liturgical experimentation, and abuses of all kinds.

Post-Conciliar Priesthood

This same climate of confusion has affected the theology of the priesthood since the Second Vatican Council. A widespread theology of the priesthood opposed the teaching of the Council and the consistent teaching of the Church throughout history. This post-conciliar "theology" of the priesthood sought to de-construct the concept of Holy Orders into a simple function of the community. Truths such as the sacerdotal character were presented as medieval constructions and the inventions of scholastic theologians.

Three examples of this faulty "theology of ministry as function," which deny the ontological character of the priesthood, can be found in the writings of Hans Küng, Edward Schillebeeckx, and Leonardo Boff.[7] Subsequently each of these three priest-theologians received official *notificatio* by the Congregation for the Doctrine of the Faith to embrace the teachings of the Church concerning the theology of the priesthood.[8] They and others taught that anyone who functioned as a priest was a priest— eliminating the need for ordination. Functional terms such as "leader" or "presider" were preferred over priestly language. "It has all been part of a general movement away from ontological (being) language in theology to a more functional (activity) approach."[9] The influence of dissident theologians is incalculable. The truth of the ontological nature of the priesthood is at stake, and this truth must be taught with clarity in a language the priests and faithful can understand. Traditional language can be employed and taught to make this doctrine of the sacerdotal character explicit. Language used by the Church must be precise because it teaches deep, spiritual truths. Either language expresses the theology of the Church, or it confuses the recipient of the spoken word.[10]

Throughout the Council a strong and relatively nuanced emphasis was placed upon the mission of the laity in the Church (*Lumen Gentium*, *Ad Gentes*, *Apostolicam Actuositatem*, and *Gaudium et Spes*), a great good in and of itself: The benefit, however, must not transpire at the expense of the ministerial priesthood. Cardinal Dulles questions the post-conciliar confusion:

> Did the [C]ouncil's teaching on the common priesthood give the laity new powers? Some

tried to use the spirit of the [C]ouncil, and
even some phrases in its texts, to argue that
it gave lay persons a kind of veto power
over magisterial teaching. Avant-garde
theologians have argued that the common
priesthood, recognized by Vatican II,
confers the right to perform certain priestly
functions, including that of consecrating the
Eucharist. But the [C]ouncil excluded these
aberrations. It taught that the common
priesthood of the faithful and the ministerial
priesthood of the ordained differ in kind
and not only in degree.[11]

In the process of conciliar *aggiornamento*,[12] some priests,
with a sincere desire to be more present and open to the
people of God, allowed the pendulum to swing too far.
With the good intention of highlighting the role and
vocation of all of the baptized, the unique role of the
ordained was neglected.

Some priests, striving to not be overly or even overtly
clerical, seemed at times *de facto* to "secularize" themselves,
while at the same time "clericalizing" the laity. Pope John
Paul II cautioned against a "[...] tendency towards a
'clericalization' of the lay faithful and the risk of creating,
in reality, an ecclesial structure of parallel service to that
founded on the Sacrament of Orders."[13] Similarly, another
theologian commented: "The temptation to clericalize
the laity by adjusting their vocation into involvement in
priestly activities should be resisted for the sake of the
integrity and dignity of the lay vocation."[14] The Body of
Christ, the Church, has many members and many parts,

and each has a role to play. To confuse those roles is to do harm to the vocations of both the clergy and the laity.

The difficulties the Church experienced immediately after the Council have left a legacy of men who have struggled to accept their specifically priestly identity. For most who have been confused, the fault is not their own, but rather the result of thirty years of ambiguity following the Council. As Pope John Paul II stated:

> [For] several generations its [the priesthood's] forms have evolved considerably; the concept of it has sometimes been shaken by the outlook of many priests with regard to their own identity; it has often been cheapened in the eyes of public opinion. [...] Today, the description of this ministry can still seem hazy, difficult to grasp by young people and lacking stability. It is thus necessary to uphold the ordained ministry. It should be given its proper place in the Church, in a spirit of communion that respects differences in true complementarity, and not one of competition that would be prejudicial to the laity.[15]

All of the Church's woes can not be blamed simply on the post-conciliar period. Those trained before Vatican II with a classical education, who nevertheless left the active ministry, give witness to problems within the priesthood even before the Council began.[16] Tragically, many men preparing for the priesthood immediately after the Council were never given sound doctrinal, spiritual, or human formation, nor were they taught about the indelible and permanent character of the priesthood; others were confused by the many conflicting theological thoughts on priestly identity in the post-conciliar period. Recently published studies show that many priests trained in this period did not understand the sacramental character of the priesthood at the time of their ordination. A substantial number of priests of that era still struggle to accept this teaching.[17]

By the late sixties, the seminaries in the United States began to experience serious problems in their programs of formation. Former rector of two major seminaries, Edwin F. O'Brien, now Archbishop of Baltimore, observed that within seminaries the following occurred: "the disappearance of the sacrosanct horarium, pastoral experiences replacing classroom academics, the de-emphasis if not elimination of philosophy, and a call for the right to theological dissent. Authoritative teaching largely became a theological note of the distant past."[18] Dr. Appleby of the University of Notre Dame explains that, for example, the systematic theology of St. Thomas Aquinas was neglected or discarded all together. "In many Catholic colleges and universities and seminaries, Thomism was supplemented or supplanted by narrative, feminist, liberationist, and other inductive theologies grounded in the communal and personal experiences of the multicultural people of God."[19]

The Lay National Review Board of the United States Conference of Catholic Bishops cited problems in the training of priests as one of the causes for the sexual abuse crisis: "in the 1970s seminaries lost their way."[20] The ordination class with the highest percentage of allegations of the sexual abuse of minors was 1970, with 10% of those ordained that year receiving accusations.[21] That period of seminary formation has been noted for deficiencies in the screening process and psychosexual formation. In the context of the 2002 abuse scandals, George Weigel noted: "If a man does not believe that what he is, by virtue of his ordination, makes the eternal priesthood of Christ present in the world, his desires may overwhelm his personality, and a life intended to be a radical gift of self can turn into a perverse assertion of self in which his priestly office becomes a tool of seduction."[22] Similarly, Weigel wrote: "A man who truly believes that he is an icon of Jesus Christ in the world, a living sacramental re-presentation in history of the eternal priesthood of the incarnate Son of God, does not behave the way clerical sexual predators behave. Focus on that, and both problems and solutions start to come into focus."[23]

This was a very difficult and confusing period in the seminary for many; it is understandable that seminarians ordained immediately after the Council were confused as to the nature and obligations of the ministerial priesthood. Archbishop O'Brien notes:

> The very meaning and identity of priesthood, along with its obligations was under discussion and debate. The institutional controls which once helped regulate, even repress affective expression from seminary and throughout ordained life evaporated virtually overnight. This opened the door to experimentation in relationships that found many leaving the active ministry for marriages and a relative handful, now in headlines [2002], whose affective immaturity proved pathological.[24]

Archbishop O'Brien continued by honoring those priests who have remained faithful despite the extremely difficult situation they found themselves in. "That so many good priests through the grace of God struggled and persevered is remarkable."[25] This should be highlighted: it is important to recognize that many good and holy priests persevered through this period of great confusion and sorrow as they saw numerous classmates leave the active ministry. As time passes, history will look back and consider these men heroes of their day. This misapprehension of priestly identity is aptly captured by Archbishop Dolan:

> The priesthood is a call, not a career; a redefinition of self, not just a new ministry; a way of life, not a job; a state of being, not just a function; a permanent, lifelong commitment, not a temporary style of service; an identity, not just a role. We are priests; yes, the doing, the ministry, is [...] important, but it flows from the being; we can act as priests, minister as priests, function as priests, serve as priests, preach as priests, because first and foremost, we are priests! Being before act! *Agere sequitur esse*, as the Scholastics expressed it.[26]

Generational Divide

A generational divide has occurred in recent years between the generation of priests trained immediately after the Council and the more recent, so-called "JP II generation." There seems to be a polarization of attitudes within the presbyterate. Many older priests fear that the younger clergy are reverting to the past and not embracing the vision or "spirit" of Vatican II. A critical caricature often painted by both groups is explained well by Bishop Gerald Kicanas. His discovery came from a recent clergy gathering discussing the topic of younger and older clergy and their perspectives of one another:

> The results were fascinating. The recently ordained saw their pastors as liberal, dissenters, socially conscious, not prayerful, wanting things done their way. And that is exactly how the pastors suspected the recently ordained viewed them. The pastors saw the recently ordained as conservative, courageous, having an exalted notion of what it meant to be a priest, pious, focused on thinking with the Pope, lacking initiative. This, too, was exactly what the recently ordained believed was the view of them held by their pastors. The discussion became rather heated when we began dialoging about the results. One of the youngest of the recently ordained cried out at one point that he had pursued priesthood at a time when his family, friends, and culture questioned why he would do that. He wanted a clear identity of what it meant to be a priest. He did not want to be one among many in the church. After all, if a lay person could do everything and was so important in the church, why should he give up so much to pursue priesthood?[27]

Msgr. Stephen Rossetti, director of the Saint Luke Institute, noted:

> [T]he candidates of today [...] come from a society that does not rejoice in their announcement of an interest in the priesthood. At best, their desire is incomprehensible; at worst, they are objects of derision. Thus, their entrance into the seminary is hard-won, at considerable personal expense. And they are reacting to a culture that is increasingly materialistic, narcissistic, sex-obsessed and functionally atheistic. Their occasional 'rigidity' is as much of a necessary defense mechanism as it is a reflection of their own need for growth.[28]

Common ground needs to be found between the two caricatured extremes: priests who are simply functionaries and priests who have a high theology of ordination. Interestingly enough, some of the disagreements between the two generations are associated with semantics, and the two extremes are not as far apart as it may seem. Studies show that both groups love the people whom they serve and enjoy preaching and celebrating the sacraments – that is why they *are* priests. Fr. Louis Cameli notes that both groups "have identifiable fears that are operative. The first group fears the demise of the renewal ushered in by the Second Vatican Council. The second group fears the dilution of tradition in some kind of gloppy, undifferentiated religiosity unanchored from its apostolic moorings." Cameli continues: "My first piece of advice to both groups is that they ought to talk with each other.

They ought not avoid each other. They should talk of substantive matters, pressing back into the vocational stories that led them to priestly mission and ministry. They will find more in common than they imagined." Cameli brings both old and new together to create a synthesis of both models. "What if we could bring together prophetic critique and attachment to tradition? Beyond the fears and suspicions of institutions and traditions, beyond the fear of the very dynamism of tradition itself we could have a powerful synthesis that could give hope and energy to the mission."[29]

The affirmation of the existence of a priestly character by those ordained since the ninety's does not necessarily imply that a pre-Vatican II attitude is returning; rather this thinking is in continuity with the tradition of the Church, the Council, and current papal teaching. The intention of this section is not to be critical of or blame priests of either generation but to allay fears of older priests regarding the "new recruits" and to encourage docility and humility amongst the younger.

Contrary to caricatures, the current generation of seminarians and new priests appear to be well-educated, mature, and ready to serve the Church and commit themselves to a life-long vocation.[30] Msgr. Edward Burns, Executive Director of the United States Conference of Catholic Bishops (hereafter USCCB) Secretariat of Clergy, Consecrated Life and Vocations, has recognized an increase in commitment among the more recent seminarians and priests, which has "been notable to rectors, formators, and vocation directors. The adjectives used to describe the men in our seminaries these days are: Courageous, dedicated, faithful, committed, loyal, spiritual – to name a few."[31] They are the next generation of priests in the United States, and they desire to be catalysts in the recovery from a crisis of priestly identity. In another example, Sr. Jane Becker, O.S.B., makes the following general observation on the population of seminarians:

> The core of the student population [… has] settled down as a less polarized group than in the eighties and a more psychologically sound group than in the seventies. The majority are simply conservative youth seeking the sacred – God, Church, commitment, and symbolization of these values.[32]

Archbishop John Nienstedt, then chair of the USCCB Priestly Formation Committee, said:

> If anything, the present seminarians are really the disciples of Pope John Paul II. They're not afraid. They've been inspired by his pontificate. They've been called to a kind of dedication and solid intellectual, spiritual and apostolic formation that he reflects.[33]

Because of the younger generation's view of the ministerial priesthood, some worry about the ability of these young clerics to work next to the laity in the diverse ministries of the Church. While priests in any age group might feel awkward or uncomfortable working with women in the Church or the laity in general, contrary to cynical opinion, studies find that this group is not particularly averse to this situation. In his study, *The First Five Years of the Priesthood*, Dr. Hoge found that seventy-three percent of younger diocesan priests were "very satisfied" with their relationships with the laity with whom they work. Another twenty-five percent were "somewhat satisfied," with their relationships with lay co-workers.[34] This means ninety-eight percent of these newly ordained priests are content in their working relationships with the laity.

While this young generation of priests seems to adapt well to diverse experiences, there is certainly the danger of the newly ordained appearing rigid or heavy handed. One mature pastor observed that a significant problem lies in the fact that:

> [...] some younger men are trying to come in and help older men do things better. They come as teacher rather than as learner, [...]. They're coming from a very legalistic mentality, a very rigid mentality as well, and also, frequently, a lack of personal sensitivity. Anyone coming into a parish needs to be pretty flexible in dealing with people, in that you have to be accepting of where people are at and then you work with them. You try to move them from where they are. To come in and think that people are going to listen to you immediately just because you are a priest is unrealistic for the most part, and some of the younger men feel that way.[35]

Experience has shown that these priests will likely mature with time and pastoral practice. Docility and humility is needed among the new generation of the presbyterate, while their elders need patience and openness to the new ideas of their younger brothers. One older priest commented: "I think, too, that the people help the priest mellow out a little and not take themselves too seriously. [...] That doesn't mean that older ones haven't been rigid, but maybe they've been in pastoral ministry long enough to be softened a little."[36] Msgr. Stephen Rossetti addresses this issue:

> In responding to these rigid candidates, I would, first of all, counsel patience. We cannot expect such mature faith, or such a deeply reconciled heart, from our seminarians or even the newly ordained. All of us go through a long process of conversion, heart-softening, and developing a pastoral heart. Let us be patient with them as others were patient with us when we first engaged in the ministry.[37]

Youthful zeal can sometimes be confused with zealotry, though in time they will learn the difference and become pastorally effective. Every priest needs to realize that the faithful will not be able to truly listen until they know they are loved by the priest. Participation in the one priesthood of Christ calls forth charity and patience.

Integration is the key for all priests, young and old alike. Dr. Luisa Saffiotti writes that priests must "avoid the 'either-or' thinking that pits commitments to social justice against fidelity to the traditions of sacramental ministry by encouraging an integrated approach, where effective work for justice is grounded in fidelity to prayer, contemplation,

Eucharist and the community of the Church."[38] Without a proper incorporation of sound theology and a spirituality grounded life, maintaining a healthy and holy priesthood will be a greater struggle. Conversion of heart on a daily basis is the key. Jesus Christ is both the reason priests are priest and the One who wants to work through them. Both groups must be called to conversion and competent theological awareness of their priestly identity.

In the minds of some, the younger generation of priests has regressed in their thinking and modeling. Hoge and Wenger comment:

> Many older priests see it as a return to the cultic model of priesthood dominant in the 1940s and 1950s, whereas many of the newly ordained see it as an innovative blend of pre-Vatican II and post-Vatican II elements into a new vision of the priesthood. [...] Whatever it [the theology of the newly ordained] is named and wherever it is headed, the second transition [since Vatican II] is a fact and an important one for the future.[39]

This newness need not be feared, Pope Benedict XVI explained to the Roman Clergy: "We must accept newness but also love continuity, and we must see the Council in this perspective of continuity. This will also help us in mediating between the generations in their way of communicating the faith."[40]

Though a natural generational divide exists as a result of priests being raised in different eras in the United States, it is unreasonable for priests to see each other in such a one-dimensional fashion. The new shift will hopefully provide a blend of identity and service. Fr. Mel Blanchette, S.S., of Catholic University of America Theological College, notes:

> The fact that this cohort of priests places more emphasis on the cultic model of priesthood does not exclude their ability to embrace the biblical notion of service that is at the heart of the priesthood. The evidence presented in the research suggests to me that cultic ministry also can embody features of the servant-leader model.[41]

It is not fair to place men of either generation in a box as though a priest cannot have a "cultic model" of the priesthood and be a great servant of the people or be a "servant-leader" and maintain an ecclesial understanding of the priesthood. Fr. Mark O'Keefe, O.S.B., encourages the continuous integration of these models; they are not opposed. "In fact, in my experience, what is usually behind what Hoge and others refer to as the 'cultic' model of the priesthood is a desire for a clear, distinctive identity. In itself, this desire is not antithetical to a spirit of 'servant-leadership.'"[42]

Many men become priests because they desire to be holy and build up the Kingdom of God. All are products of their environment and training; all sides need to let go of "baggage" and move forward so that priestly fraternity can be restored in every presbyterate. It is time to refocus on exactly what the Church teaches regarding the ministerial priesthood and not allow the popular, cultural context in which formation occurred define the priesthood.

The Hermeneutical Key

Understanding the origins of the labels of servant-leader and the sacral/cultic model are important for future discussion. The hermeneutical key to understanding these models is in the writings of Cardinal Avery Dulles, S.J. For too long the theology behind these models has been taken out of its proper context, and it is crucial for the presbyterate to rediscover its true meaning rather than distort the original intention of Dulles, the heart of which emphasizes the sacramental character as the foundation of the priestly life.

Avery Dulles, born in 1918, has been one of the leading theologians in the United States during the past forty years.[43] In his arguably most famous work, *Models of the Church*, originally published in 1974 (revised in 1986 and again in 2002), he presented five "models" or approaches through which the Church may be understood.[44] The five models of the Church are: Church as Institution; Mystical Communion; Sacrament; Herald; Servant. He also developed parallel models of priestly ministry within the Church: "five models of ministry."[45] Regarding that model which was most critiqued in the 1970s, the "sacramental [sacral or cultic] view of the priesthood," he wrote: "Catholicism has perhaps a special responsibility to keep alive this sacral dimension of the priesthood."[46] In his doctoral dissertation on Cardinal Dulles, Fr. Robert Spezia noted:

> It is possible to misread *Models of the Church* in at least two ways. The first is to take each model in isolation. [...] A second way to

misread *Models of the Church* is to assume
that Dulles favors the model that he treated
last. This is the servant model. Again, this
would be an incorrect interpretation. Avery
Dulles has stated that his intention is to hold
these models together in tension since they
all contribute elements of the total truth of
the Church's mystery.[47]

This is an extremely important point regarding his five
models of ministry because the "servant-leader model"
prevailed in the period following Vatican II to the detriment
of the "sacral model" of ministry. Each of these models
emphasizes a different aspect of the ministerial priesthood;
thus, the priest is called to be a man of the institutional
Church, a man of communion, a sacred mediator, a herald
of the Good News, and a servant leader, as Dulles noted:
"These functions do not exclude one another, but they stand
in some mutual tension."[48] Each of these aspects of ministry
is important and should not be taken as individual models
but as part of a greater reality – the priesthood of Jesus
Christ. However, since the priest as "sacred mediator" is of
particular importance in this book, Dulles will be quoted
at length regarding the positive and negative attributes of
this model:

A great deal of the strength of Roman
Catholicism over the past few centuries has
come from the attraction of this sacramental
view of the priesthood. This image of the
priest leads to a high sacerdotal spirituality,
and is felt to be helpful to many of the laity.
If office in the Church is not to be a merely

secular thing, but is to lead to an authentic encounter with God, the symbolic and mystical dimension of the priesthood should not be neglected. The bishop or pastor should not be allowed to turn into a mere business manager or personnel officer.

Like every good thing, however, the sacral concept of the priesthood can be exaggerated. It can lead to a superstitious exaltation of the priest as a person possessed of divine or magical powers. He may become removed from the rest of the community and surrounded with an aura of cultic holiness more redolent of paganism than of Christianity. Various clerical practices may contribute to this distortion – for example, the stress on living apart, on special garb, on a special sacred language, and on mandatory celibacy. The danger is that the priest will be viewed as a substitute for the community – as one who stays close to God so that the laity, relying on his intercession, may be worldly. This is a reversal of what is, of course, intended: namely, that the priest be holy in order to lead the community to holiness, prayerful in order to gather up their prayer, learned so as to give them understanding, and so forth.

In Roman Catholicism today we are witnessing a full-scale revolt against the excesses of the sacral concept of ministry. Rejection of this stereotype is one of the sources of the present vocation crisis in the Church. Still there are valid elements in this controverted view. The official

representative of the Christian community
needs to be united to God in prayers and
faith, well versed in the Scriptures, and
ready to sacrifice himself, as Christ was, in
the service of others. As a focal center for the
community the priest must visibly be a sign
and sacrament of Christ. Catholicism has
perhaps a special responsibility to keep alive
this sacral dimension of the priesthood.[49]

Because of an unbalanced reading of his models by
some theologians, Dulles has had to emphasize in his
various writings the sacral dimension of the ministerial
priesthood.[50]

Throughout his writings he has emphasized the
importance of the sacramental character of the priesthood
as the basis upon which to build an understanding of the
ministerial priesthood, while integrating all of the other
dimensions as well. In 1977, worried about the danger of
functionalism, he wrote:

The liberals make it too easy for themselves
because they neglect the sacramental aspect
of the priesthood. In my own view, the
permanent commitment of the priest and
his undivided consecration to the work of
the Lord is a powerful sign of God's active
transcendence and of the surpassing value of
what Jesus calls the "pearl of great price." To
do away with priesthood in the traditional
sense and to substitute a ministry conceived
in purely functional terms is scarcely an
advance. I do not believe that the priest who
looks upon the vocation as just another job

> – perhaps even as a temporary or part-time
> occupation – can personally symbolize the
> total commitment of the Church to Christ
> its Lord.[51]

Dulles stressed the importance of the understanding of permanence in the priesthood during a period of time when certain theologians were calling for radical reforms (as seen earlier in this chapter). He, of course, never turned away from the idea that the priest is also the servant-leader, an important facet of the ordained ministry.

In a talk delivered in 1990, he revisited his five models of the Church and further expounded upon their parallel ministerial models. He offered a synthesis of what he had already written and called it a synthetic, unitive, or representational model of the priesthood. Dulles explains: "Christ gives his priests authority to represent him – to speak and act in his name."[52] The priest re-presents Christ to the community through his very person and through the sacramental acts of his ministry. Dulles then offered the synthesis of this model:

> This "representational" model is more
> closely related to the sacramental model of
> the church than to any of the other four.
> But, unlike the previous five models of the
> priesthood, this model is not specifically
> linked with any one type of ministry. It
> penetrates beyond functionalism to what
> may be called an ontology of priesthood.
> Sacramentally representing Christ as
> the head of the church, the ministerial
> priesthood expresses itself not only in prayer

and worship, but in all the activities that the bishop or presbyter performs in the person of Christ as head.[53]

In other words, the priest is always a priest. Dulles further explains:

> The term 'representative' calls for some clarification, since it is frequently used to mean a mere substitution of one person for others. In theology, however, the idea of representation is not juridical but organic. The priest is configured to Christ in order that Christ may act in him as an instrument.[54]

He is not just configured to or representing Christ in the performance of the sacraments; rather, because of ordination he always acts *in persona Christi*.[55] More recently he has straightforwardly written:

> [T]here is some debate among contemporary authors about whether the priestly character is ontological or merely functional. In accordance with authoritative teaching on the nature of episcopal consecration, it seems that the character imparted must be in some sense ontological: it is a consecration affecting the new priest in his very being. But the character is also functional in the sense that it is dynamic; it imparts a radical capacity and aptitude to perform certain acts. Metaphysically, I suppose, the character could be described as a spiritual quality, and more technically as a *habitus*, belonging to the supernatural order.[56]

Dulles undeniably believes the priestly character indelibly marks the priest and that this fact is an important theological starting point to then understand the radical service he is to render. Lest he overemphasize the ontological identity of the priest and undervalue the subjective responsibility of the individual, Dulles, like von Balthasar, focuses on the importance of the priest cooperating with God's grace to lead a holy life.[57] Even though the priest is conformed to Christ through the sacramental character, he needs to allow the Holy Spirit, through prayer and virtuous living, to transform him further.

> To be transparent to Christ, as his vocation requires, he must prayerfully live up to his vocation and frequently "rekindle the gift of God" that is in him through the laying on of hands (cf. 2 Tim. 1:6). When and to the extent that he lives up to the grace of his calling the priest may be said, in a certain sense, to be "another Christ." The maxim, "He who hears you hears me" is applicable. The priest's sense of identity is secure to the extent that he has faith in the sacrament and relies on the grace of ordination.[58]

The priest needs to be a credible witness to an evangelical way of life.[59] He should be a living sign of the love of God in the world by the way he treats his flock. His sense of identity is secure to the extent that he understands the gift he has received and responds to that gift. The proper knowledge of "who one is" as a son of God and a priest of Jesus Christ should lead to the faithful fulfillment of the office of the priesthood.

Avery Dulles offers the Church a sound theology of the ministerial priesthood through his writings on the "representational model." Because of the ontological change at ordination, the priest sacramentally re-presents Christ to the Church – *agit in persona Christi capitis*. Utilizing Cardinal Dulles' ideas on the truth upheld by the Church regarding priestly character provides the necessary perspicuity to foster a growing unity among priest of all generations.

The Essence of Priesthood

The two notions, one functional and the other sacral, are often seen in competition with one another; in fact, they are at the service of one another. The priest is called to be aware of his sacred role as one who has been sacramentally sealed at ordination, and flowing from his consecration, he is to be a servant-leader and shepherd of the flock of Christ. The truth represented in *Presbyterorum Ordinis* supplies the balance needed for today's priests. In this decree explicit reference is made regarding the priest in relation to the Body of Christ as the one who re-presents Christ (*in persona Christi capitis*). Following this, the primary theme of the same document is that of the priest following the example of the Good Shepherd.[60] The emphasis is first on who the priest is (ontologically) and then on what he does, namely that the good shepherd "lays down his life for the sheep" (Jn. 10:11).

Regarding the pastoral service owed to the people of God, Pope Benedict XVI reminded seminarians: "Always keep before your eyes the figure of Jesus, the Good Shepherd, who 'came not to be served but to serve, and to give his life as a ransom for many' (Mt. 20:28)."[61] He clarifies that service to the people of God is the reason behind the character. As Cardinal Ratzinger, he explained:

> This means that the ontological conception of the priesthood, reaching into the being of the interested person, is not opposed to the seriousness of the functional activity of the social aspect of the priesthood, but rather creates a radicalness in serving which would be unthinkable in a purely profane activity.[62]

The representation model Dulles offers reminds the priest he is always a priest and to allow Christ to inform all he does in the sacraments and in the service he offers the Church. He is *in persona Christi* as a good shepherd who lays down his life for the sheep. According to recent studies, priests who understand and integrate a proper perception of their ontological identity into life and ministry appear to be more faithful and joyful servants of Christ and His Church. Secular sociologists have shown in their studies:

> On every measure, the priests with a cultic ecclesiology reported more happiness, less inclination to leave the priesthood, and a higher percentage saying that if they had to do it over again, they would become priests again. [... In contrast] the servant-leader-type priest had lower morale and more thoughts of resigning. Our best guess is that possibly they felt a less distinctive priestly identity, providing them less self-affirmation and esteem."[63]

As evidenced in these studies, there is an apparent correlation between men with a strong sense of priestly identity and finding deep contentedness in their lives.

This finding is crucial for the future of priestly vocations. The witness of priests joyfully living their vocation is essential for reclaiming the gift of the priesthood today and fostering vocations for the future. Pope John Paul II wrote in *Ecclesia in America*: "Bishops and priests are particularly responsible for encouraging vocations by personally presenting the call, and above all by their witness of a life of fidelity, joy, enthusiasm and holiness."[64] Similarly, the 2002 Instruction from the Congregation for the Clergy stated: "Personal example, given by visibly owning his priestly identity [cf. *DMLP* 66], living consistently with it, [...] and catechesis on the ordained ministry are indispensable to any pastoral promotion of priestly vocations" (*PPLP* 22). Essentially, a more theologically grounded understanding of the essence of the priesthood is crucial if vocations are to be discovered, nurtured, and properly developed.

Given the documented evidence of tensions between older and younger priests, the need to bridge this gap by means of a renewed sense of fraternal respect and a fidelity and openness to the teachings of the Church is necessary. Priests need to focus more on what they hold in common in their mission to serve Christ, rather than stress only the differences. Hoge and Wenger found "many areas of agreement: all agreed on their love for God's people, desire to serve God's people, love for the Catholic Church, desire for personal fulfillment [...] not everything is polarized."[65]

The crisis and conclusions described in the landscape described above are undoubtedly real. Yet out of this turbulence and confusion, genuine renewal of the priesthood remains possible. Priests must confidently embrace the vocation God has bestowed on them. This certainly does not mean priests are better that the laity whom they are called to serve, but they are different by virtue of their ordination. Priests standing in the midst of the world unapologetically distinct, the studies show a greater contentedness in their lives. Sr. Susan Wood, S.C.L., acknowledges these findings: "According to the data, this strong identity promotes greater clerical happiness and stability. Those espousing this view of the priesthood have fewer thoughts of leaving the priesthood. A larger number would choose the priesthood again, given the option. Role clarity and visibility seem to strengthen the priesthood."[66]

In the recent epoch of the Church a renewed understanding that priestly spirituality and identity go together has developed. Possessing a deep knowledge of his identity allows the priest a greater ability to respond to God's grace in daily priestly activities. A greater sense of identity should lead to a happier, healthier, and more fruitful living out of the priesthood. There is a mutual correspondence between a proper understanding of the priestly character and growth in spirituality, and spirituality solidifies identity. Integrated spirituality serves to strengthen the priest's sense of identity. The sacramental character is the foundational aspect of the priestly life of love and service. The next chapter will look at some practical principles and repercussions of this foundation.

Notes

1 Benedict J. Groeschel, C.F.R., *From Scandal to Hope* (Huntington, Indiana: Our Sunday Visitor, 2002), 20.

2 "Vatican II: The Myth and the Reality," *America*, 24 February 2003, 8.

3 Pope John XXIII, "*Gaudet Mater Ecclesia,*" *L'Osservatore Romano*, 12 October 1962, 1. He announced the Council to a group of Cardinals at the Basilica of St. Paul on January 25, 1959 (*AAS* 51 [1959], 65-69), and prayed on 23 September 1959, that this would be a "new Pentecost" for the Church (*AAS* 51 [1959], 832). It is attributed to Pope John that he said: "I want to throw open the windows of the Church so that we can see out and the people can see in."

4 George A. Kelly, *The Battle for the American Church Revisited* (San Francisco: Ignatius Press, 1995), 16.

5 George Weigel, *The Courage to be Catholic: Crisis, Reform, and the Future of the Church* (New York: Basic Books, 2002), 62.

6 Cardinal Dulles wrote: "The difficulty was increased by the condition of the Western culture in the years when the council was being received. In the Western world the dominant liberalism impelled the interpreters to fit the council's teaching into the prevailing democratic and egalitarian categories. Publicists of the council, moved by the spirit of the times, often gave tendentious readings to the documents. When they could not successfully twist the text to suit their own purposes, they appealed to the spirit (or the style) and ignored the letter. [...] As a result, everything came to be placed on the same level: Christianity and other religions, the Catholic church and other Christian communities, the hierarchy and the laity, the sacred and the secular" ("Vatican II: Substantive Teaching," *America*, 31 March 2003, 15).

7 Commenting on the first two theologians, and others like them, Dulles wrote: "Questioning the doctrine that any 'indelible character' was imparted by sacramental ordination, they suggested that service for a period of years, and even part-time service would be appropriate. Influenced by modern democratic ideologies, some denied that there was an essential difference between the common priesthood of the baptized and the ministerial priesthood of the ordained. In an emergency situation, they contended, the congregation could select one of its own members to preside at worship and even offer the Eucharist. [...] Proposals of this kind, especially when backed up by the authority of prominent writers such as Hans Küng and Edward Schillebeeckx, made a great impact" ("The Priest and the Great Jubilee," *The Priest*, June 1998, 33). For a sample of their writings see Hans Küng, *Why Priests?: A Proposal for a New Church Ministry*, trans. Robert C. Collins, S.J. (Garden City, New

York: Doubleday, 1972), 63-64 and 88-95; Edward Schillebeeckx, *Ministry: Leadership in the Community of Jesus Christ* (New York: Crossroads, 1981), 72-73 and 138-138; and Leonardo Boff, *Ecclesiogenesis: The Base Communities Reinvent the Church*, trans. Robert R. Barr (Maryknoll, New York: Orbis Books, 1986), 70-75.

8 Cf. "Vatican Declaration on Father Hans Kueng," *Origins* 4 (6 March 1975): 579; "Vatican Congregations Letter to Bishops: The Minister of the Eucharist," *Origins* 13 (15 Sept. 1983): 231-232; "Vatican Letter to Father Schillebeeckx: Who Can Preside at the Eucharist?" *Origins* 14 (24 Jan. 1985): 525; "Notification on L. Boff's *Church: Charism and Power* – Doctrinal Congregation Criticizes Brazilian Theologian's Book," *Origins* 14 (4 April 1985): 683-687; and "Franciscan Father Leonardo Boff, a Brazilian Liberation Theologian, Has Been Removed, *Origins* 21 (30 May 1991): 42.

9 Michael Evans, "*In Persona Christi* – the Key to Priestly Identity," *The Clergy Review* 71 (April 1986): 118.

10 "A shift of terminology accompanied the functional vision. One avoided using the words 'priest' or 'priestly' on account of the sacral meaning; in its place one used the neutral-functional term 'minister' which at the moment had almost no importance in Catholic theology" (Ratzinger, "Life and Ministry of Priests," in *Priesthood: A Greater Love – International Symposium on the Thirtieth Anniversary of the Promulgation of the Conciliar Decree Presbyterorum Ordinis*, 28 October 1995, 77-78).

11 "Vatican II: Substantive Teaching," 16.

12 Philip Trower explains *aggiornamento* to his readers thus: "Making Catholics more fervent and apostolic, and the faith better understood by outsiders, would also, it was believed, be advanced by the process Pope John [XXIII] called *aggiornamento*, translated into English as 'updating' or 'renewal'" (*Turmoil and Truth: The Historical Roots of the Modern Crisis in the Catholic Church*, [San Francisco: Ignatius Press, 2003], 11).

13 Cf. John Paul II, *Christifideles laici: Post-Synodal Apostolic Exhortation on the Lay Members of Christ's Faithful* (Vatican City: Libreria Editrice Vaticana, 1988), 32.

14 Thomas J. McGovern, *Priestly Identity: A Study in the Theology of Priesthood* (Dublin: Four Courts Press, 2002), 90.

15 "Confront the Crisis in Vocations Prayerfully and Practically – *Ad limina Apostolorum*: Bishops' Conference of France – 2," 6 December 2003, *ORE*, 10 December 2003, 19. The Pope was speaking to the French bishops regarding reasons why it is difficult for young men to consider a priestly vocation.

16 "But, behind the grand-looking façade of religious practice, there

must have been something amiss, something in need of reform. Catholics [especially priests] do not suddenly abandon large numbers of their beliefs and moral principles if they have been serving God as they ought. [...] Another weakness could be faith and piety without an adequate depth and breadth of theological understanding [and integration] or of current theological speculation and problems" (Trower, *Turmoil and Truth: The Historical Roots of the Modern Crisis in the Catholic Church*, 46, 48).

17 Cf. Dean R. Hoge and Jacqueline E. Wenger, *Evolving Visions of the Priesthood: Changes from Vatican II to the Turn of the New Century* (Collegeville: Liturgical Press, 2003), 58. Also by Dean Hoge, *The First Five Years of the Priesthood: A Study of Newly Ordained Catholic Priests* (Collegeville: Liturgical Press, 2002) and *Experiences of Priests Ordained Five to Nine Years* (Washington, D.C.: NCEA, 2006). Cf. also, Stephen H. Louden and Leslie J. Francis, *The Naked Parish Priest: What Priests Really Think They're Doing* (London: Continuum, 2003); "A Survey of Roman Catholic Priests in the United States and Puerto Rico Conducted by the Los Angeles Times Poll June 27 to October 11, 2002," *Los Angeles Times* (www. latimes.com/home/news/polls [downloaded 17 March 2004]).

18 Edwin F. O'Brien, "Reformation of Catholic Seminaries," *The Priest*, June 2002, 19. While Archbishop of the Military Services, U.S.A., O'Brien was given the task of episcopal oversight for the Apostolic Visitation of all seminaries and houses of formation during the academic year 2005-2006.

19 R. Scott Appleby, "Surviving the Shaking of the Foundations: United States Catholicism in the Twenty-First Century," in Katarina Schuth, O.S.F., *Seminaries, Theologates, and the Future of Church Ministry: An Analysis of Trends and Transitions* (Collegeville: Liturgical Press, 1999), 4-5. However, the documents of Vatican II as well as the Code of Canon Law have affirmed St. Thomas as the model for theology in the seminary, "in order to throw the fullest light on the mysteries of salvation, let the students learn, with the aid of speculative reason under the guidance of St. Thomas, to penetrate them more deeply and see their mutual connection" (*OT* 16; *CIC* 252 § 3). Regarding traditional Thomistic philosophy and theology, Pope John Paul II reminded the Church of the importance of St. Thomas in philosophical and theological studies, "It should be made clear in the light of these reflections why the Magisterium has repeatedly acclaimed the merits of St. Thomas' thought and made him the guide and model for theological studies. [...] The magisterium's intention has always been to show how St. Thomas is an authentic model for all who seek the truth" (*Fides et Ratio: Encyclical Letter on the Relation Between Faith and Reason* [Vatican City: Libreria Editrice Vaticana, 1998], 78). The demise of the Thomistic concepts of substance, accidents, and essence

has contributed to theological confusion.

20 "John Jay Report," 3.3 (John Jay College of Criminal Justice, "The Nature and Scope of the Problem of Sexual Abuse of Minors by Catholic Priests and Deacons in the United States (1950-2002): A Research Study Conducted by the John Jay College of Criminal Justice" [www.usccb.org/nrb/johnjaystudy/exec.pdf (downloaded 27 February 2004)].

21 Ibid.

22 *The Courage to be Catholic*, 175.

23 "From Scandal to Reform: (Part 1)" www.eppc.org (downloaded 29 May 2003): 4.

24 Edwin F. O'Brien, "Reformation of Catholic Seminaries," 20.

25 Ibid.

26 *Priests for the Third Millennium* (Huntington, Indiana: Our Sunday Visitor, 2000), 228. Pope Benedict XVI, then as Cardinal Ratzinger, illuminates the error of priestly identity as function: "Indeed, when the distinction is made, there generally is a suggestion that the word orthodoxy is to be disdained: those who hold fast to right doctrine are seen as people of narrow sympathy, rigid, potentially intolerant. In the final analysis, for those holding this rather critical view of orthodoxy everything depends on 'right action,' with doctrine regarded as something always open to further discussion" ("Eucharist, Communion ands Solidarity," *ORE*, 13 Nov. 2002, 6)

27 "Toward a Renewed Priesthood," in Hoge and Wenger, *Evolving Visions of the Priesthood*, 152-153.

28 "The Priest as Man of Communion," in *Vocation Journal 2002* (Little River, South Carolina: NCDVD, 2002), 59.

29 Louis J. Cameli, "Apostolic Hope," (Archdiocese of Chicago: Priests' Convocation, 30 June 2005, photocopied), 12. "To understand this [new] generation is to understand their trust of the institutional life of the Church and the way they prize tradition" (ibid., 11).

30 For instance: "57% had graduated from college with a bachelor's degree before entering seminary; 20% had earned a master's degree before seminary; 3% a doctorate; 2% had previously earned law degrees" ("Ordination Class 2002 Shows More Priests from Mexico, Vietnam," *NCDVD News* [Fall 2002]: 21). Critical articles in the November and December 2006 issues of *Commonweal Magazine* have dispute the educational levels of today's seminarians. As one who has taught in a theologate, I disagree and feel the men today to be bright and eager to learn the Church's teaching in order to share it with the faithful.

31 "Sociological and Cultural Issues Affecting Priestly Vocations," *The Priest*, November 2006, 18.

32 "A Word from the Seminary World: Today's Candidates and Their Issues," in *Priesthood 2000: Developmental and Human Resource Perspectives* (Chicago: NFPC, 1999), 29. Writing of the psychological well-being of this group, Sr. Katarina Schuth offers the following insights: "Most seminarians enter theology physically and psychologically healthy, with sufficiently outgoing personalities to conduct the public ministry required of the Church's ordained. Faculty describe most of them as earnest, pious, and committed. They enter consciously into a formation process that asks them to accept criticism and to change their behavior and attitudes in conformity with the expectations of priesthood" (*Seminaries, Theologates, and the Future of Church Ministry: An Analysis of Trends and Transitions* [Collegeville: Liturgical Press, 1999], 86-87). Fr. Stephen Rossetti agrees with these findings regarding the health and balance of this younger generation. He stated: "the bulk of the candidates for the priesthood today are solid psychologically and spiritually" ("The Need for Connections," in Hoge, *The First Five Years of the Priesthood*, 133).

33 Ellen Rossini, "Pope to Church: Risky Seminarians Must Go," *National Catholic Register* (15 September 2002), as found on www.opusbonosacerdotii.org/ncr2.htm (downloaded 18 September 2003).

34 Cf. Hoge, *The First Five Years of the Priesthood*, 23 and 168.

35 Hoge and Wenger, *Evolving Visions of the Priesthood*, 74-75.

36 Hoge and Wenger, *Evolving Visions of the Priesthood*, 76.

37 "The Priest as Man of Communion," 59.

38 "Forming Ministers for the Twenty-First Century," *Human Development*, Summer 2005, 10.

39 Hoge and Wenger, *Evolving Visions of the Priesthood*, 113.

40 "'Choose Life' Means Choosing God," *ORE* 15 March 2006, 8.

41 "Understanding Self as Key to Spiritual and Human Development," in Hoge, *Experiences of Priests Ordained Five to Nine Years*, 133.

42 "Initial and Ongoing Priestly Formation," in Hoge, *Experiences of Priests Ordained Five to Nine Years*, 169.

43 Cf. Dulles, "*Curriculum Vitae*." One need only look at his degrees, credentials, and the honors that he has received during the past forty years to see the esteem and respect with which he is held not only in the United States but also in the Church Universal. He was "created" a Cardinal of the Church on January 21, 2001 (Dulles, *Curriculum Vitae*, www.fordham.edu/dulles/cv.htm [down-loaded 24 February 2003]).

44 Dulles, *Models of the Church: Expanded Edition* [New York: Image Books, 2002], 26-94. Donovan comments: "In his well-known and influential 1974 *Models of the Church*, [...] Dulles developed an approach to ecclesiology

that focused on five different and finally complementary 'models' that people were using more or less consciously when reflecting on the nature and mission of the church" (*What Are They Saying about the Ministerial Priesthood?*, 134).

45   Cf. Dulles, *Models of the Church*, 152-166.

46   Ibid., 160.

47   "The Ecclesiology of Avery Dulles, S.J. – A Hermeneutical Key" (S.T.D. diss., Pontifical University of St. Thomas Aquinas [Rome], 2003), 19-20. Spezia wrote in the footnote to the quote above: "In an interview this writer had with Avery Dulles on September 11, 2001, Dulles confirmed that he most prefers the sacramental model" (ibid.).

48   *Models of the Church*, 166.

49   Ibid., 159-160. Donovan commented on Dulles' desire to emphasize the sacral model: "While sympathetic to the rejection of abuses and exaggerations, he was concerned lest the reaction go too far" (*What Are They Saying about the Ministerial Priesthood?*, 134).

50   Cf. Ibid., 152-153; "*Successio Apostolorum – Successio Prophetarum – Successio Doctorum*," *Concilium*, vol. 148, *Who Has a Say in the Church?* (New York: Seabury Press, 1981): 61-67; *A Church to Believe In: Discipleship and the Dynamics of Freedom* (New York: Crossroad, 1982), 151-152; "Models for Ministerial Priesthood," *Origins* 20 (Oct. 11, 1990): 284-289; *The Priestly Office: A Theological Reflection*, 7-15; "Gender and the Priesthood: Examining the Teaching," *Origins* 25 (May 2, 1996): 779.

51   Dulles, *The Resilient Church: The Necessity and Limits of Adaptation* (Garden City, New York: Doubleday & Co., 1977), 41-42. Avoiding any semblance of functionalism, Dulles wrote: "It could happen, however, that through illness, imprisonment or some other contingency, a priest would go for years without performing actions specifically proper to the ministerial priesthood. He would not for that reason be any less a priest, for the priesthood permanently bestowed by ordination itself, penetrates the whole life of the priest in the church" ("Models for Ministerial Priesthood," 288). Spezia (218) noted: "The sacramental model has occupied the heart and apex of [Dulles'] thought on *Models of the Church*. [... The] sacramental model has been Dulles' most favored model."

52   Dulles, "Models for Ministerial Priesthood," *Origins* 20 (Oct. 11, 1990): 288.

53   Ibid., 288. Dulles went on to say: "In speaking of the 'indelible character' the church expresses both the permanence of the priesthood and its impact on the very being of the ordained. They become in a new way ecclesiastical persons – that is to say, public persons in the church" (ibid.).

Dulles writes that some functions of the priest can be legitimately performed by laypersons, "[b]ut when performed by priests they take on, so to speak, greater ecclesial density. They come to be attributable, though in varying measure, to the church as such" (ibid.).

54 *The Priestly Office: A Theological Reflection*, 14.

55 "Dulles' position [regarding ontology] has affinities with the interpretation that John Paul II has given to the phrase *in persona Christi*. [...] The sacramental representation of Christ is meant to permeate all that priests do 'in the person of Christ the head'" (Donovan, *What Are They Saying about the Ministerial Priesthood?*, 136-137).

56 Dulles, *The Priestly Office: A Theological Reflection*, 12.

57 Hans Urs von Balthasar (1905-1988) emphasized both character and worthiness: the objective transmission of the office of the priesthood and Christian discipleship need to be integrated in such a way that there is no fracture in the credibility of the office. Von Balthasar wrote that there must be unity in the life of Christians – who they *are* and what they *do* – for both clergy and laity alike. Ultimately all priests must wrestle with the "dualism that exists between their objective ministry [*Sein*] and their subjective commitment [*Sollen*] – between office and person [...]" (*The Christian State of Life*, trans. Sr. Mary Frances McCarthy [San Francisco: Ignatius Press, 1983], 267; cf. also 306, 315-321, 274-276). One cannot divorce *Sein* and *Sollen*. They are both essential to the credibility of the priesthood. *Sein* without *Sollen* can fall into the dangers of clericalism, and *Sollen* without *Sein* can fall into the trap of functionalism. For further commentary on von Balthasar see Dermot Power, *A Spiritual Theology of the Priesthood: The Mystery of Christ and the Mission of the Priest* (Washington, D.C.: CUA Press, 1998), 94-96. Von Balthasar died on June 26, 1988, just two days before he would have received the "red hat" from Pope John Paul II at the consistory in Rome (cf. Peter Henrici, S.J., "A Sketch of Von Balthasar's Life," *Hans Urs Von Balthasar: His Life and Work*, ed. David L. Schindler [San Francisco: Ignatius Press, 1991], 41).

58 Dulles, "Models for Ministerial Priesthood," 288.

59 Dulles, like von Balthasar, emphasizes embracing the "evangelical counsels" for secular clergy as well. "Priests themselves will often be unduly influenced by values contrary to their vocation. But those who prayerfully and joyfully dedicate themselves to the evangelical counsels provide a powerful witness to a greater love, thereby inspiring the whole Church to a more authentic following of the Gospel" (Dulles, "The Priest and the Great Jubilee," 38).

60 Cf., *PO* 3, 5, 6, 9, 11, 13, 14, 18, and 22.

61 "The Church: 'Security and Consolation' For All Believers," *ORE*, 16 May 2007, 12.

62 "Life and Ministry of Priests," in *Priesthood: A Greater Love* –

International Symposium on the Thirtieth Anniversary of the Promulgation of the Conciliar Decree Presbyterorum Ordinis, 28 October 1995, 121.

63 Hoge and Wenger, 124 -126.

64 *Ecclesia in America: Post-Synodal Apostolic Exhortation on the Encounter with the Living Jesus Christ: The Way to Conversion, Communion and Solidarity in America* (Boston: Pauline Books and Media, 1999), 40. (ibid., 40).

65 *Evolving Visions of the Priesthood*, 114.

66 "The Search for Identity," in Hoge and Wenger, *Evolving Visions of the Priesthood*, 169.

Chapter 3

The Foundation of the Priestly Life:

Principles and Repercussions

Six key themes or principles can be enumerated regarding the Church's teaching on the sacerdotal character. Each of these principles forms a part of the whole: different aspects of the one mystery. First, a central element of the priestly character is permanence. Second, the priest acts *in persona Christi* in the dispensation of the Sacraments, which are efficacious and gracious gifts of Christ to the Church. Third, the priest also acts *in persona Ecclesiae* in the exercise of his duties. Fourth, the priest's presence and authority are a gift to the faithful because it comes from the very core of his being. Fifth, mere functionalism must be avoided. Sixth, ongoing formation is essential for the priest to recognize the gift he possesses.

Taking a scholarly approach to characterizing the landscape of the priestly identity and exploring the depths of theological possibilities always involves a risk of over-theorizing and understating the possibility of practical applications. Although many angles to the ideas here presented need to continue developing, there is an urgency to provide some practical guidelines to help redirect toward or preserve an authentic identity of the priesthood. Flowing from each of the principles mentioned above are ramifications or repercussions for priestly living. These principles and repercussions certainly are not an exhaustive list but a sufficient start to reveal that the teaching of the sacerdotal character is indeed the foundation of priestly life and ministry.

As seen in the previous two chapters, Pope John Paul II was evidently convinced that, to fulfill their ministry, priests must have a clear notion of their identity. To reiterate the point, note what he pleaded in 1982 to a group of priests:

> [...] with all the power of persuasion at my command I say to each one: priest, *be what you are*; without restrictions, without illusions, without compromise in the face of God and your conscience; [...] be that in the stature of your personality, in your way of thinking and loving. Have always and clearly *the courage of the truth of your priesthood.* Let no shadow obscure that light that is within you. Let no detour distance you from the structure of your sacred character.[1]

In this same address, the Pope pointed to the "ontological and irreplaceable necessity" of the ministry of the priest, and he stressed "the mystical identification 'in the person of Christ,' which is our primary *raison d'etre*." He continued: "Today I wish to confirm you, strengthen you, root you ever more deeply in that *sacred reality* which constitutes the essence of the priest."[2]

John Paul II asked his priests: Why do you doubt your own identity?

> This high and exacting service cannot be carried out without a clear and deep rooted conviction of your identity as priests of Christ, depositories and administrators of God's mysteries, instruments of salvation for men, witnesses of a kingdom which begins in this world but ends in the next. In light of these certainties of faith, why doubt about your own identity?[3]

Following St. Peter himself, Pope John Paul II, during his twenty-six year pontificate, cried out to his priests: "Be solicitous to make your call and election permanent, brothers; surely those who do so will never be lost" (2 Pt. 1:10).

As the second chapter of this book has shown, many priests doubted their identity in the decades following the Second Vatican Council. This doubt or denial stemmed from several factors, including the social climate of the day, poor theological formation, and even outright dissent from the Church's teaching regarding the ministerial priesthood. In the midst of this, the Church constantly held to the theological and practical importance of the sacramental character of the priesthood. These factors prompt the continuing need for clear, guiding principles, but also for practical suggestions with immediate value to pre- and post-ordination formation.

If a priest truly understands the theological richness of who he has become at ordination, certain manifestations of that doctrine should be seen or evidenced in his life and the way he lives his priestly ministry. Because the fullness of priestly character was underrepresented by a particular number of theologians after the Second Vatican Council, many practical consequences were likewise jettisoned, jeopardizing priestly identity itself. "A necessary condition for the formation of an authentic priestly identity is sufficient [and] accurate knowledge of the church's teaching especially about sacramental priesthood." This knowledge and formation must also be interiorized: "Internalized behaviour [...] is a unifying factor as attitudes and actions become personal convictions that are integral to the personality, manifestations of the actual and ideal self, and expressions of the person's deepest identity."[4] When the priesthood is lived out in the integrity of its fullness, it is a great gift to the People of God and meant to edify the Church.

The practical conclusions offered here are external signs pointing to the priest's understanding of his interior reality. These practical principles are vital in providing a more robust framework of priestly identity, not only for the formation of seminarians, but also for priests in need of exploring and re-envisioning their value to the Church and the parishes they serve.

First Principle: Permanence of the Priesthood

You are a priest forever!
(Ps. 110:4; Heb. 5:6)

The first principle is the permanency of the priesthood. Through ordination, priests receive a sacramental character, which indelibly marks their soul. Acknowledging the permanent nature of this character serves to remind priests of their life-long union, commitment, and relationship with Christ and His Church, and that Christ has also entered into a permanent relationship with them. Pope Benedict XVI said: "At the moment of your ordination, through the imposition of hands, Christ took you under His special protection; you are concealed under His hands and in His Heart. Immerse yourselves in His Love, and give Him your love!"[5] The priest should grow in this loving, personal, and enduring relationship for the whole of his life. Christ loves His priests, who stand in His Person, and this relationship should bring the ordained into deep union with Him as they serve the needs of the world. Fr. Greshake wrote: "It is indelible because it is effected by the unbreakable promise and unchanging will of Christ to transmit [H]is work of salvation through the ministry of the ordained."[6] The repercussions of this permanent and loving relationship follow analogously along the lines of a marital relationship: namely, engagement, marriage, and parenting.

Actively Engaged

First of all, as a young man begins to hear the call of Christ deep within (i.e. falling in love), he explores the possibility of following Him as a priest. As this discernment continues, he applies to a diocese or religious order and eventually begins his seminary formation to find out if he has a priestly vocation. The seminary is *the* place to discern; a commitment has not yet been made, and years of formation will occur before a decision is necessary. However, at some point the seminarian must accept this vocation as his own through prayer and spiritual direction or leave the program of formation to pursue other avenues of serving God in this life. It is dangerous for a man preparing for Holy Orders to vacillate between leaving and staying during his last few years of formation. He must internally commit at some point; for if he is always discerning priesthood, he is not being formed for the priesthood. At a certain point, discernment must cease and formation and commitment take precedence. (A similar problem happens to couples who cohabitate – it hinders their decision process in preparing for permanency in marriage.)

Fr. George Aschenbrenner, S.J., wrote of this problem in his book, *Quickening the Fire in Our Midst*. He dedicated an entire chapter to this issue entitled, "Presumption for Perseverance and Permanence."[7] Aschenbrenner questions whether priests who left active ministry truly understood what they were promising at ordination and whether their seminary preparation integrally prepared them for living the sacerdotal ministry in today's world.[8] He stated that a true sense of the life-long commitment must come into the formation program much earlier than right before diaconate. The degree of commitment of some seminarians is insufficient to meet the state of life for which they are being prepared – they never entered into a period of "active engagement." "Though this presumption of permanence cannot be made too early, backing it up too close to diaconate ordination also destroys its effectiveness. Ideally, the presumption spoken of here should be made at least a year or two before diaconate ordination."[9] The candidate who has not assimilated this presumption for permanence is in grave danger. "In [such instances] the candidate does not learn the important process of living discerningly in the light of a God-given identity and mission, a process that is meant to become the very inner structure of his life after ordination."[10] Integration of theology and spirituality is, at times, lacking in the lives of seminarians. Such a lack inhibits their capacity to more permanent commitment. Archbishop Dolan commented on this, stating: "the number one priority in the formation of candidates for the priesthood for the ministry of the new evangelization is the development of a vibrant, durable, and sustaining spiritual and intellectual life."[11]

Aschenbrenner makes the point that an integrated mindset and a priestly self-understanding serve as a "rudder" to guide the rest of priestly ministry after ordination. With this in mind, the seminarian recognizes that at ordination he will make a permanent commitment to the Eternal Priesthood of Christ.

> Seminary preparation is not simply directed toward the exciting event of ordination

but rather toward the lifelong identity and ministry of the priesthood. [...] The rite of ordination is an act of God in and through the church. [...] As publicly ratified in the church, it has a certitude and clarity that can stay with the priest through the rest of his ministry. This presumption, tested and ever more assimilated over the years, now stands as a rudder, a compass, a beacon giving light, balance, and direction for the future.[12]

The promulgation of clearly defined formation models is essential if those in formation are expected to integrate and interiorize the life-long commitment made at ordination. Aschenbrenner explains that actively engaging in the formation process and committing oneself is not easy for today's generation:

[...] contemporary culture has so enthroned autonomy and self-fulfillment that it is hard to talk about commitments that can perdure beyond intensely self-absorbed feelings and projects. Add to these cultural aspects the contemporary postmodern development [...] and the possibility of permanent commitment seems even more dismal. [...] Such belief in the radical changeability of self affects even the possibility of a permanent profession of this "self." In some cases, as in postmodernity, the permanent profession of self is outright denied; in other cases the denial is more subliminal but no less real.[13]

In other words, without a solid theological integration and understanding of the sacramental character as a foundation for the seminarian regarding the permanence of the ministry, he could be easily led away from his vocation by either discouragements or temptations after ordination. "The presumption of priestly permanence presented here should play a central role in seminary preparation. If the candidate does learn such presumption, it will make a difference in his preparation for petition for priestly ordination. It will also aid him in the joys and trials of priestly ministry."[14]

This is especially necessary for the current generation, many of whom grew up in homes that have suffered pain and confusion from separation and divorce. These factors have further intimidated young people today regarding permanent commitments; they are simply afraid. Msgr. Edward Burns[15] recognizes the fear of commitment as a substantial societal problem:

> Increasingly, lack of commitment contributes to the declining number of men entering the seminary. A number of reports and statistics suggest that it is not only the priesthood in the Catholic Church that shows a decline in the numbers, but that the [number] of ministerial leaders in other denominations are also decreasing. Interestingly, a number of denominations are experiencing fewer clergy, even those that call to ministry married men as well as women. It seems that the solutions some prescribe for the lack of priestly vocations (e.g., optional celibacy) would not address the real issue of lack of commitment. North America faces a commitment crisis, not a vocation crisis. Even marriage suffers from the lack of commitment in our society;

recently the Washington Post reported that marriage is at an all time low.[16]

The young people of our time, who experience this fear, are to be encouraged to grow as disciples of the Lord and grow in trust of His will for their lives, whether they are called to marriage, priesthood, consecrated life, or remain in the single state.

Pope John Paul II was aware of these postmodern trends and their impact on the current generation. He cautioned a group of bishops, during their 2003 *Ad Limina* visit, that the youth of today have a great "fear of long-term commitment, for there is a fear of taking a risk for an uncertain future, and we live in a changing world where interests seem ephemeral and essentially linked to instant gratification."[17] Likewise, his successor, Pope Benedict XVI, spoke a similar message to the young:

> Young people are very generous, but when they face the risk of a lifelong commitment, be it marriage or a priestly vocation, they are afraid. [...] Reawaken the courage to make definitive decisions: they are really the only ones that allow us to grow, to move ahead and to reach something great in life. They are the only decisions that do not destroy our freedom but offer to point us in the right direction. Risk making this leap, so to speak, towards the definitive and so embrace life fully [...].[18]

Seminarians able to make this presumption for perseverance and permanence well in advance of ordination enter into a period of engagement with the Church, their Bride-to-be, which allows them to freely commit to and prepare for their life-long and permanent commitment.

Chaste Spouse [19]

A seminarian lacking a deep desire for marriage and children needs to rethink his vocation, for these manly desires of the heart are natural and healthy. He needs to recognize that, in actuality, the priest truly *is* a married man and a father. The Sacrament of Matrimony is the foreshadowing of the marriage of Christ and the Church (cf. Eph. 5), a marriage the priest *in persona Christi* enters into. Therefore, the natural analogy of marriage used for the priest and the Church is in no way fictitious but real. As with faith, the supernatural is more real than the natural: Baptism is more of a true birth, the Eucharist is the most nourishing food, Reconciliation is the deepest forgiveness, Confirmation is the full reception of Trinitarian Life, Anointing of the Sick is the most core healing. So the supernatural marriage of the priest to the Church is the real prefigurement of the heavenly kingdom where "they neither marry nor are given in marriage" (Mt. 22:30). This is the chaste, spousal love in which every soul will find its fulfillment in heaven. This kind of chaste spousality the priest enters into is not un-natural, as many say today, but it is super-natural – a call by God to belong totally to Him, body and soul, in this life in anticipation of the life to come.

As the priest has been configured to Christ through ordination, he shares in a a love for the Bride of Christ in a more profound way; the priest thus enters into a nuptial relationship with the Church. "Husbands love your wives, even as Christ loved the church and handed himself over for her [...]" (Eph 5:25). What is Christ's is his own; therefore, the priest must lay down his life for the Church and understand that he has entered into a relationship, like marriage, for the whole of life. "The priest is called to be the living image of Jesus Christ, the Spouse of the Church" (*PDV* 22). Pope John Paul II had a particular affinity for this image of the priest as bridegroom:

> Therefore, the priest's life ought to radiate this spousal character which demands that he be a witness to Christ's spousal love, and thus be capable of loving people with a heart which is new, generous and pure, with genuine self-detachment, with full, constant and faithful dedication [...] (*PDV* 22).

> The Church as the Spouse of Jesus Christ, wishes to be loved by the priest in the total and exclusive manner in which Jesus Christ her Head and Spouse loved her. Priestly celibacy, then, is the gift of self *in* and *with* Christ *to* his Church and expresses the priest's service to the Church and in the world (*PDV* 29).

Understanding that priests are not simply bachelors is important. The priest who has the mindset that he is in a permanent relationship with Christ and His Church will not live as a bachelor or absentee-father; rather he will commit himself wholeheartedly to his family of faith. Otherwise, rather than enjoying the fulfillment of what is gained, there is a danger of focusing on what is lost. Fr. Aschenbrenner warns priests about this "bachelor syndrome." He wrote:

> Bachelors, feeling that the challenge and the vigor of life have passed them by, usually become uninvolved spectators. In self-protection, they often radiate a superior, critical attitude and condescendingly carp at people who are seriously involved with the challenges of life. Undue concern with their own security and hypochondriacal fear for their own health are often further symptoms of this bachelor syndrome.[20]

The priest has entered into a permanent, loving, and covenantal relationship with Christ and His Church, and not understanding the spousal nature of the priesthood brings consequences that undermine his fulfillment in this life.

Through the discipline of celibacy in the Latin Rite of the Church, the priest is to be a committed bridegroom.[21] John Paul II stated: "The priest must be faithful no matter how many and varied the difficulties he meets, even in the most uncomfortable situations or when he is understandably tired, expending all his available energy until the end of his life" (*PDV* 75). McGovern affirms: "[...] the priest's spousal relationship with the Church is an integral part of his identity."[22] The priest, in spousal relationship with the Church, is called to be generative by his love. His self-gift is to be fruitful for the life of the Church, his bride, the Bride of Christ. Pope John Paul's "Theology of the Body" speaks to this reality in which the consecrated celibate can be "understood positively as 'conjugal' that is, expressed through the total gift of oneself."[23] On the practical level, this affects the way a priest must guard his affections. He is a married man who has given himself to a Bride. He is to be attentive to her and not give his heart to any other, but to love and give himself completely to her. In this self-offering, he receives. The priest lives in open and active receptivity with God, Who fills him, while at the same time he is pouring himself out for his loved one. If he is to avoid becoming a bachelor, he must love and allow himself to be loved by his Bride, the people of God. Only thus will he be able to unite himself fully with Christ in the words of consecration: "This is my body, which will be given up for you."

Spiritual Father [24]

Just as parents will do anything for the good of their children, so too will priests sacrifice for the good of their spiritual family. Thus the priest is rightly called "father" of the family of faith, a title he should not dispense with or take lightly.[25] Vatican II speaks of both the bishop and the priest as fathers of the Church. "Like fathers in Christ, they are to look after the faithful whom they have spiritually brought to birth by baptism and by their teaching (see 1 Cor. 4:15; 1 Pt. 1:23)" (*LG* 28). The priest's understanding of himself as "father," serves as a reminder of both his permanent relationship and full-time commitment to his spiritual family.

Fr. Evans notes: "The fatherly model of ministry is also a useful one [...] to express the permanent rather than purely functional role of the priest in the Church." He continues:

> It seems to me that 'father' is a particularly
> good form of address which expresses well
> the combination of real leadership and
> loving care which should be the hallmark of
> a priest's ministry. In my own experience, it
> is not the form of address that is divisive but
> rather the manner of exercising one's spiritual
> fatherhood.[26]

Dr. Scott Hahn takes this understanding one step further: "A priest must be a man who knows he is a father, and knows that his fatherhood is something real, something metaphysical, something theological, and something permanent."[27] The priest's vocation is to be faithful to his spouse and available to his children as *pater familias* (cf. *PPLP* 19 and *DMLP* 58). Archbishop Timothy Dolan commented on the notion of fatherhood as connected to the understanding of ontological permanence: "People call us, not 'Reverend,' not 'Doctor,' not 'Vicar,' but 'Father' – and 'Father' is an identity based on being, not on function."[28] Dolan wrote elsewhere:

> They call us 'Father,' and look to us for the
> love, care, and wisdom such a title implies.
> Our people know that priesthood is more
> than a job, a profession, a career, or even a
> ministry; they know that priesthood is a life,
> an identity, a permanent call that changes our
> very being.[29]

Speaking of the kind of mature manhood needed to face this paternal challenge, Pope Benedict XVI squarely states:

> In reality, we grow in affective maturity when
> our hearts adhere to God. Christ needs priests

who are mature, virile, capable of cultivating an authentic spiritual paternity. For this to happen, priests need to be honest with themselves, open with their spiritual director and trusting in divine mercy.[30]

The spiritual paternity of the priesthood is real, sharing in the same joys and sorrows of every family: as he baptizes and buries, as he witnesses marriages and counsels them in failure, as he laughs and at times cries with all of the people that come to him as father, seeking *the* Father's love and care. Recognizing the fruitfulness and generativity of his life through his spiritual children is a source of genuine joy for the priest. His life of love and service is indeed fecund and so beyond him. He realizes he is a vessel – a conduit for the Father to make the Son through the Holy Spirit present in the world. Through this he does not suppress his virility but allows God to use him, and in turn he experiences the joy of spiritual fecundity.

Essentially, this first principle suggests that the gift of priesthood is a lifelong, permanent undertaking. He is called to offer himself as a "living sacrifice" (Rom. 12:1) for his spouse, the Church (cf. Eph. 5:22-32). At the consecration when the priest says, "This is my Body," not only is he offering the Body of Christ to the world, he is offering his own life as a sacrifice for the Church. Therefore, permanence of the priesthood – developing a spousal relationship with and for the Church and allowing his fatherhood to shape his day-to-day ministry – represents one of the most fundamental principles of priestly identity.

Second Principle: In Persona Christi

And behold, I am with you always, until the end of the age.
(Mt. 28:20)

The priest has been sealed and ontologically changed through ordination for a specific purpose: so that he can make Christ sacramentally present to the faithful. This theme focuses specifically on the *munus sancitficandi* of the priest (cf. *PO* 5). The priest has been deputed to act (*deputatio*) and sent on mission (*missio*) by Christ: "Do this in memory of me" (cf. Lk. 22:19). He has been consecrated in order to consecrate and sanctify the faithful through the sacraments. One theologian explained it thus:

> St. Thomas defined the character as a deputation to cult, which empowered the ordinand to act in Christ's person in the administration of the sacraments. He also brought out very clearly that the character was a relation to the visible church, which enabled the recipient to posit acts which are acts of the ecclesial community. While St. Thomas spoke only of the liturgy, what he said can be extended to all of the priest's pastoral activities. [...] [T]he Vatican Council showed how all of the actions of the ministry may contribute to that worship of God which is a holy life, lived in acceptance of the Gospel. It is because he is made Christ's representative through reception of the character that the priest exercises all his pastoral activity, of word and government as well as of sacrament, acting in the name and person of Christ.[31]

The priest is called to integrate who he became at ordination with a way of life that is worthy of his calling, so to edify and not scandalize the Church.

Efficacious Character

The ministerial priest receives the *deputatio* to act *in persona Christi capitis* in the sacramental life of the Church. The sacraments are valid and efficacious whenever a priest celebrates them. The doctrine of the character offers such an assurance of the objective nature of the mysteries of the faith, avoiding reliance on the subjective disposition of the priest. This offers the people of God great comfort in knowing that, despite the unworthiness and, at times, even sinfulness of the priest, the sacraments are efficacious because of the indelible character he possesses. This indelible character gives the faithful the assurance of the validity of the sacraments.

If a priest performs the sacraments while in a state of serious sin, those sacraments are valid; however, he damages the state of his own soul.[32] Reflecting this Thomistic thought, Pope Benedict XVI, then as Cardinal Ratzinger, wrote: "The character guarantees the 'validity' of the sacrament even in the case of an unworthy minister, being at the same time a judgment on him and a stimulus to live the sacrament."[33] Thus, the sacraments are valid *ex opere operato*. Patrick Dunn wrote: "Perhaps the most striking feature of the doctrine of sacramental character is that it gives structural stability to the Church. Without it the visibility of the Church and the value of the Liturgy and the Eucharist would all be undermined."[34]

Christ thus remains present with His Bride until the end of time. The sacraments are efficacious signs of His gracious love for the Church. Christ comes through the ministry of the priest to cleanse (Baptism), nourish (Eucharist), strengthen (Confirmation), forgive (Reconciliation), unite in love (Matrimony), and heal (Anointing of the Sick). The priest who recognizes this mystery within himself cannot but gratefully and humbly live his calling. As he stands in the person of Christ, the priest is the instrumental cause of the sacraments and, likewise, has need of being fed as he feeds and healed as he heals. He recognizes both the power and efficacy of his ministry and his radical dependence on Christ through the same sacraments.

Something not well understood today is the need priests and the world have for the daily celebration of the Eucharist. If priests have a proper appreciation of the sacerdotal character and of the efficacy of the Holy Sacrifice of the Mass, they will, even on their day off, offer Mass, which is the defining or *"essential moment of their day"* (*PDV* 48). In 1993, Pope John Paul II spent the greater part of the year dedicating his Wednesday audience catecheses to the ministerial priesthood. On June 9th the Holy Father's talk was entitled, "Priests: Spiritually Rooted in the Eucharist." John Paul II believed so firmly in the ontological nature of the priesthood that he encouraged the celebration of the Eucharist even when the faithful are not gathered together. This seems absurd to those who do not believe in the efficacious and meritorious nature of the Mass.

> If the priest 'hears' this truth proposed to him
> and to all of the faithful as the voice of the

New Testament and Tradition, he will grasp the Council's earnest recommendation of the 'daily celebration (of the Eucharist), which is an act of Christ and the Church even if it is impossible for the faithful to be present' [*PO* 13]. The tendency to celebrate the Eucharist only when there was an assembly of the faithful emerged in those years [after Vatican II]. According to the Council, although everything possible should be done to gather the faithful for the celebration, it is also true that, even if the priest is alone, the Eucharistic offering which he performs in the name of Christ has the effectiveness that comes from Christ and always obtains new graces for the Church. Therefore, I too recommend to priests and to all the Christian people that they ask the Lord for a stronger faith in this value of the Eucharist.[35]

In 2003, in his fourteenth encyclical letter, *Ecclesia de Eucharistia*, the late Pope also wrote:

We can understand, then, how important it is for the spiritual life of the priest, as well as for the Church and the world, that priests follow the Council's recommendation to celebrate the Eucharist daily: 'for even if the faithful are unable to be present, it is an act of Christ and the Church' [*PO* 13 and *CIC* 904].[36]

There is no such thing as a "private" Mass, since it is always an action of the whole Church: both militant and triumphant. Blessed Columba Marmion explained that even a missionary "in the depths of the bush does not say *Orem* [let me pray] but *Oremus* [let us pray]. It is in the name of the whole of Christendom that he sends up his prayer to God."[37] Granted, celebrating alone is not the ideal, but the value in the gift of the celebration of the Eucharist is such that the priest should never fail to offer it for the needs of his people and the whole world.

Likewise, concelebration at the Eucharist is an efficacious action of the priest. Every Mass offered by the priest, even as a concelebrant, has infinite value. By virtue of ordination, the priest has a proper role in the Liturgy distinct from that of the laity. The *General Instruction of the Roman Missal* states that "it is preferable that priests who are present at a Eucharistic Celebration, unless excused for a good reason, should as a rule exercise the office proper to their Order and hence take part as concelebrants, wearing the sacred vestments."[38] As Msgr. K. Bartholomew Smith has noted:

> The unity [of the priesthood] that is emphasized by the rite of concelebration comes from the ministerial character of the priesthood, in that each and all priests act as instruments of Christ the one High Priest whenever they celebrate the Eucharist [cf. *Ecclesiae Semper: Decree on Concelebration and Communion under Both Species*, 5 and 8]. [...] Ordination changes forever the relationship of the recipient to the Church in general and the Eucharist in particular by setting him apart to offer sacrifice in the High Priesthood of Christ. Just as a baptized Christian fails in his duty not only to himself but to the rest of the people of God if he does not exercise his

communion, so does the priest fail not only himself but the whole Church if he does not fulfill his sacramental function.[39]

There are intentions that need to be prayed for as each priest is united to the Lord in the Mass, even as a concelebrant. The priest's role in the life of the Church is indispensable and one which he should not flee from with a misconstrued notion to promote the democratization of the Church, thus denying his identity. To paraphrase Pope John Paul II: Priest, be who you are!

The focus on the sacramental character allows a balance to be maintained between the "objective ministry and subjective commitment."[40] Cardinal Walter Kasper comments that "precisely this 'ontological' understanding is a help and a consolation [to priests], because they can say to themselves that the salvation of their communities and of the people committed to them does not ultimately depend on their own accomplishments and their own success. This is a consolation as well for many communities."[41]

Character Development

The acceptance of the truth that the priest stands *in persona Christi* may be jeopardized if it is not lived in integrity. Due to scandal in the Church, many have had their faith shaken regarding the nature of the priesthood. While the sacraments are not dependent upon the worthiness of the minister, the priest has a subjective responsibility to respond to the gift received at ordination. For the sake of God's people, the priest must foster his personal character and align it with the sacramental character received at ordination so he may be a credible witness to the One who sent him. Fr. Federico Suarez writes: "Each individual must behave in accordance with what he is. The priest, a consecrated man, has a special quality, the quality of something holy, for his sacramental consecration endows him with a sacred character. He can no longer behave as if this special quality did not exist. He is a man of God, belonging no longer to himself but to God alone."[42]

The moral implications that apply to the Baptized gain further weight in light of the character of the priesthood.

> The word [character] has also been used in ethics to indicate that morality is to be understood not just in terms of doing right actions, but, at a deeper level, in terms of virtue, the consistent conduct of a personal agent whose mind and will are fixed on a supreme good, so that moral action comes to him [...] almost as "second nature," as we say. [...] The priestly character is the personal reality corresponding to the outward matter and form of ordination. The comparison between this spiritual character and the moral character should be kept in mind.[43]

The efficacy of the sacraments dispensed by the priest and the objective reality of the Sacrament of Order he has received demand an integration of living and being the gift received at ordination. The Congregation of Clergy explains: "This commitment is made concrete in a profound *unity of life* which leads the priest to be and live as *another Christ* in all the circumstances of his life"[44] Fr. Galot further explains:

"This means that, more so than the ordinary Christian, the priest is called to take Christ as his model in all his behavior."[45] The priest is certainly not better than anyone else, but because of his state of life as an ordained witness to Christ, the call to holiness is elevated and the obligation to be a man of extraordinary virtue is inherent. Indeed, the people of God have a "right" that their priests strive to live lives of holiness. Priests have an obligation to respond to the call to lead a holy life (cf. *CIC* 276 § 1). The Bishops of the United States agree:

> Because of the ministry entrusted to priests, which in itself is a holy sacramental configuration to Jesus Christ, priests have a further reason to strive for holiness [*PO* 12]. This does not mean the holiness to which the priest is called is in any way subjectively greater than that to which all the faithful are called in virtue of Baptism. While holiness takes different forms, holiness is always one [*LG* 41]. The priest, however, is motivated to strive for holiness for a different reason: so as to be worthy of that new grace which has marked him so that he can represent the person of Christ, Head and Shepherd, and thereby become a living instrument in the work of salvation [*PO* 12].[46]

Priesthood requires of a man a moral character resonant of the dignity of the sacramental character within him. Likewise, the sacred mysteries he celebrates, offered reverently and with devotion, witness his profound respect before the Lord and assist the faithful in their journey.

The man who has received the mission to stand *in persona Christi capitis* is called to be a credible witness to the faithful in both *sacred character* and *moral character*.[47]

The recent, unusually high rate of unethical behaviors and scandals reported in the media across so many sectors (political, educational, corporate, and ecclesial) cause concerns about potential fissures in adult moral character. Consequently, the tendency to restore formation efforts in moral character and human development, particularly for adults, has been growing. Although formal research across multiple disciplines may have neglected the construct of moral character development, the media has consistently upheld its relevance. Although media sensationalism may lead to disingenuous conclusions and generalizations, it always remains possible to extract lessons from popular journalism. Notably, while sex scandals in public office are considered a personal character flaw, their occurrence, even among a minority of priests, results in widespread distrust of the entire priesthood. The underlying assumption is that being a religious figure automatically implies a high degree of moral character. Despite this common assumption, being religious offers no guarantee for strength of character. Therefore, the urgency to look at moral character is much more manifest in the Roman Catholic Church in the United States since the sex scandals.

Developing his character during seminary years and post-ordination is vital in establishing a healthy framework of priestly identity. The revised Program of Priestly Formation emphasizes the importance of character:

Applicants must give evidence of an overall personal balance, good moral character, a love for the truth, and proper motivation. This includes the requisite human, moral, spiritual, intellectual, physical, and psychological qualities for priestly ministry (PPF 44).

The same document explains that the sacramental character builds on the moral character of the human person, which must be ever open to greater conversion in Christ:

In virtue of the grace of Holy Orders, a priest is able to stand and act in the community in the name and person of Jesus Christ, Head and Shepherd of the Church. This sacramental character needs to be completed by the personal and pastoral formation of the priest, who appropriates "the mind of Christ" and effectively communicates the mysteries of faith through his human personality as a bridge, through his personal witness of faith rooted in his spiritual life, and through his knowledge of faith (PPF 237).

The Program for Priestly Formation (hereafter PPF) elaborates on exactly the kind of moral character the Church is looking for in candidates for Holy Orders: "*A person of solid moral character with a finely developed moral conscience, a man open to and capable of conversion*: a man who demonstrates the human virtues of prudence, fortitude, temperance, justice, humility, constancy, sincerity, patience, good manners, truthfulness, and keeping his word, and who also manifests growth in the practice of these virtues" (PPF 76).

Moral character is refined and purified through ongoing conversion and frequent use of the Sacrament of Reconciliation and spiritual direction. Blessed Columba Marmion suggests frequent use of the Sacrament of Reconciliation to help the priest advance toward this ideal. He voices his concern for those who do not. "I am convinced that priests who make it a practice to confess only at intervals of many weeks, or even many months, are wanting in supernatural prudence. [...] By confession only at rare intervals a priest sacrifices precious graces of sanctification and exposes himself to grave danger of falling into a state of tepidity."[48]

The gift of the priesthood rests on the validity of the sacraments, as the priest acts in persona Christi. At the same time, the sacerdotal character should be a stimulus for men to grow in moral character by virtue of the dignity and responsibility of the priestly vocation.

Third Principle: In Persona Ecclesiae
This makes us ambassadors for Christ,
as if God were appealing through us.
(2 Cor. 5:20)

By virtue of ordination, the priest not only stands *in persona Christi*, he ministers *in persona* or *in nomine Ecclesiae*; he no longer represents just himself.[49] He first represents Christ; therefore, he represents His Church. "In exercising their specific functions, they act *in persona Christi Capitis*, and consequently, in the same way, they act *in nomine Ecclesiae*"

(*PPLP* 6).[50] Through the Church and the ministry of Her priests, Christ is made present in the world sacramentally. The priest is in relationship to the Church because he is first in relationship with Christ as His minister. Sr. Sara Butler noted: "It is because he acts *in persona Christi capitis* that he is able to act *in persona Ecclesiae*."[51] Fr. O'Keefe wrote:

> Ordination, then, is not basically an empowerment by the Church to act on its behalf (as some theologians argue), but it is an empowerment by God to represent Christ as Shepherd of the Church, and *therefore* to represent the Church. That God is the principal agent of ordination, through the invocation of the Holy Spirit, is clear in the ordination rite itself. The ordained priest acts *in persona ecclesiae* (in the person of the Church) because he first acts *in persona Christi capitis*, because of the distinct way that he is related to Christ.[52]

Essentially, he does not possess priestly authority because he is a functionary of the Church but because of the sacramental character configuring him to Christ the High Priest. Since the priest represents the Church as Her official representative, however, he is obligated to pray for Her and make Her visibly present in the world today.

The Liturgy of the Hours

Because the priest primarily represents Christ the Head of the Church, he also speaks in the name or person of the Church: *in persona Ecclesiae*. The priest, then, is called to be the voice of the Church and to intercede for the needs of the people of God. Next to the Eucharist, the most efficacious way he prays for the Church is through the recitation of the Divine Office. The great liturgical theologian, A. G. Martimort, noted that the obligation for priests to faithfully recite the *Liturgy of the Hours* "emanates from the very nature of their mission and the sacramental character impressed upon them."[53] The priest has been ontologically changed so that he can stand *in persona Christi capitis* before the people of God and *in persona Ecclesiae* before God Himself. The *General Instruction of the Liturgy of the Hours* states that priests "are themselves representative in a special way of Christ the Priest, and so share the same responsibility of praying to God for the people entrusted to them, and indeed for the whole world."[54] A priest who understands his identity will not fail in his promise to pray the Liturgy of the Hours *in persona Christi et Ecclesiae* for the needs of God's people.[55] In 2002, the Congregation for the Clergy reiterated the *serious* obligation of the priest to daily pray the *Liturgy of the Hours*,

> an obligation he freely undertook *sub grave*. [...] The priest has received the privilege 'of speaking to God in the name of all,' indeed of becoming almost 'the mouth of the Church.' In the Divine Office he supplies what was lacking in the praise of Christ and, as an accredited ambassador, his intercession for the salvation of the world is numbered among the most effective (*PPLP* 14).[56]

Archbishop Dolan makes the claim: "I contend that the renewal in the priesthood for which we all long will not occur until we return to a fidelity to the promise we made as deacons to pray daily with and for the Church in the Divine Office."[57] The priest who knows who he is – the ambassador of the people before the throne of God – takes seriously the promises made at ordination to pray faithfully the Liturgy of the Hours. While the recitation of the *Liturgy of the Hours* by the faithful is encouraged, as it is the "prayer of the Church," the ordained minister has publicly promised to officially pray it for the needs of the whole world.

Pope Benedict XVI calls praying the *Office* a "free space" to enter and present ourselves before the Lord and intercede for the souls entrusted to us:

> As people of prayer, we represent others when we pray and in so doing, we fulfill a pastoral ministry of the first order. This is not to withdraw into the private sphere, it is a pastoral priority, it is a pastoral activity in which our own priesthood is renewed, and we are once again filled by Christ.[58]

The promise made at ordination to pray the *Liturgy of the Hours* is about relationship – relationship with God and with the faithful. Not uncommon or surprising, a man who leaves the active ministry inevitably admits he has not prayed the Office for quite some time. The obligation of the priest to recite the Office serves as a constant reminder of God's presence, the needs of the people, and a way to sanctify the whole of his day. The five times he is called to enter into this "free space" offers him moments to recollect himself and, even if brief, to "taste" the Lord's presence and recognize Him in the midst of death and struggle. At times this sacred duty may seem burdensome, but as the priest goes beyond himself and picks up the Office, it is always a moment of grace for him and the Church.

Blessed Columba Marmion counseled priests thus:

> Certainly the recitation of the Office is a great exercise of faith; we do not see the results of our efforts or of our prayer. [...] What does God expect of His priests? The generosity to spend themselves for the salvation of souls certainly; but this giving of self must be made fruitful by the recitation of the breviary. You must be convinced of this.[59]

To help priests who struggle with the recitation of the Office, he advises a few moments of preparation spent recollecting what is about to happen and to Whom one is about to speak. "Without preparation, the breviary will inevitably be recited nonchalantly, mechanically."[60] Blessed Marmion also recommends having particular intentions for which to pray during the Liturgy of the Hours:

> It is an excellent practice to form an intention which will serve as the motive for our recitation. It is easier to keep our minds alert when we have before our eyes the reasons which urge us to pray. Before we begin, let us think of the sufferings and dangers of so many souls; of the multitude of sinners, this immense mass of humanity harassed by demons and vice. When we forget ourselves in this way, we can feel that we are the *os totius Ecclesiae*, and experience the inspiration of devotion.[61]

The priest who knows who he is will not shirk this pastoral duty or the spiritual grounding the Breviary offers to his day. As a chaste spouse and spiritual father, he offers his time and prayer in *nomine Ecclesiae* for the people of God.

Visible Sign

The priest is always a priest. "He is priest continuously, internally, invisibly; he is a priest always and at every moment, whether he is performing the highest and most sublime office or the most vulgar and humble action of his ordinary life."[62] He not only represents Christ, he also represents the whole of the Church. Therefore, the presence of Christ and the image of the Church should be manifest primarily by the actions of the priest, but also in a visible way. The most simple and evident way this is done is by being visibly recognizable as a priest.

> For a priest to dress in lay attire is to disguise the fact that his very *raison d'être* is to draw souls to Christ. He has a representative role which is, as a consequence of ordination, part of his very being. To dress as a priest is to give witness to the total commitment of one's life and to manifest the presence of Christ among men.[63]

Though at times it may be uncomfortable or inconvenient, the priest who does not fail to wear his collar will find himself an instrument of God in ways otherwise unimaginable. "The indelible character, imparted on the soul by the sacrament of Order, cannot be privatized because it was given by the

Church for the service of others. The faithful [...] have a need of the sign value of a priest dressed as a priest."[64]

The 1994 *Directory on the Ministry and Life of Priests* encourages priests to be attentive to this detail of their lives as public witnesses of Christ and His Church:

> In a secularized and materialistic society, where the external signs of sacred and supernatural realities tend to disappear, it is particularly important that the community be able to recognize the priest, man of God and dispenser of his mysteries, by his attire as well, which is an unequivocal sign of his dedication and his identity as a public minister. The priest should be identifiable primarily through his conduct, but also by his manner of dressing, which makes visible to all the faithful, indeed to all men, his identity and his belonging to God and the Church. [...]
> Because of their incoherence with the spirit of this discipline, contrary practices cannot be considered legitimate customs [...]. Outside of extremely exceptional cases, a cleric's failure to use this proper ecclesiastical attire could manifest a weak sense of his identity as one consecrated to God (*DMLP* 66).[65]

Not only does the Roman collar allow the priest to foster simplicity of life, it allows him to be ever more a servant of all. It is more a form of asceticism than of clericalism if worn with humility and service as the driving force and is a visible sign of the radical commitment of the priestly life. In the *Directory* (and subsequent *Dubium*) the Church is simply reminding Her priests that failure to dress as a priest "could manifest a weak sense of [priestly] identity." This does not mean the priest must wear the Roman collar twenty-four hours a day, for certainly there are moments of rest and recreation when it will not be necessary or appropriate.[66]

In the best sense, priests need to be proud of who they are and who they represent: Christ and His Church – to "reclaim their priestly character." As the *Directory* states, the priest leads primarily through the way of life, but that life must be made visible in the world today in tangible ways. Msgr. Stephen Rossetti writes in *The Joy of the Priesthood*:

> While the external signs of the priesthood may facilitate the process [of renewed identity], such signs will not be fully effective unless we priests, and the laity, are able to complement these external signs with an inner appropriation of a unique priestly identity.[67]

The exterior must mirror the interior reality and disposition of a true servant of the Lord. The people of God are thirsting to see visible signs of God's presence in the world today. To see a Roman collar around the parish, in the airport, at the store, at a restaurant, around town – wherever the priest is present – is a comfort and a reminder of God's presence. The visible priest is always an eschatological sign pointing beyond himself. Priests who avail themselves in this way experience the extraordinary joy of their fatherhood in the ordinary moments of daily life.

The priest is certainly not his own, and this belonging to Christ and living in the heart of the Church shapes his spirituality and entire existence in and for the world. The priest is a living sign of Christ's presence to His people: clerical attire reminds the priest to appropriate his identity interiorly and gives hope to the people exteriorly that "Christ" is still with them; fidelity to the Liturgy of the Hours serves as an efficacious means to live fully and attentively each moment of the day. Thus, the gift of praying and living *in persona Ecclesiae* is a joyful duty for the priest who knows who he is and Whose he is.

Fourth Principle: Priestly Presence

I live, no longer I, but Christ lives in me; insofar as I now live in the flesh, I live by faith in the Son of God.
(Gal. 2:20)[68]

The ontological change wrought at ordination occurs in the very depths of the priest's soul; a change occurs in his soul. The sacerdotal character provides a power the priest may not always even be aware of, a power not limited to the cultic dimension of his ministry – in a unique way his presence makes Christ present. In the Gospels, as Christ healed and taught, the people were amazed because he taught with power and authority: *exousia* (cf. Mt. 7:29; Mk. 1:22; Lk. 4:32; Jn. 7:15ff). As stated above, *exousia* literally means that one's actions and authority come "from one's being." Since the priest's soul has been configured to Christ, he participates in Christ's authority; his very being allows Christ to be present in a unique way. *Ultimis Temporibus*, in 1971, stated: "This authority does not belong to the minister as his own: it is a manifestation of the Lord's *exousia*, or power, by which the priest is an ambassador of Christ in the eschatological work of reconciliation (cf. 2 Cor. 5:18-20)" (*UT* I, 5). This theme deals specifically with the other two *munera*: *docendi* (or *propheticum*) and *regendi* (cf. *PO* 4 and 6). The priest speaks with the authority of Christ; he should have confidence in the power of his teaching, preaching, shepherding, and healing, for in them, Christ is present.

Preaching

A large part of the priest's life and ministry is the proclamation of the Word. Liturgical preaching is a moment the priest can engage his people and offer them hope and life as he opens up the Sacred Scriptures.

> By virtue of his character, the priest participates equally in the sacerdotal power of Christ, the messenger of the Father to men. The New Testament seems to include in the priesthood the apostolic ministry of the word (Rom. 15:16) [... The preaching of the priest *qua* priest has] an objective, sacred character, inalienable, a quasi-sacramental radiation.[69]

The priest speaks with the authority and presence of Christ, and he should have confidence in the power of his preaching. Fr. George Aschenbrenner, S.J., wrote: "True preaching focuses, with an inspirational ring of authority, on the fire of God's love in Jesus and springs from the priest's whole experience of living, praying, and acting in the person of Christ [...]."[70]

The Church invites only her ordained ministers to preach at the liturgy. The *Code of Canon Law* states: "The most important form of preaching is the homily, which is part of the liturgy itself, and is reserved to a priest or deacon" (*CIC 767*).[71] This is not to say laypersons cannot be eloquent in proclaiming the Gospel message (very often they are more so), but in the context of the liturgy, the ordained are commissioned to be the official preachers of the faith. According to Pope Benedict XVI, the Liturgy is to be viewed as a whole: "Delivering the homily during Holy Mass is a task bound to the ordained ministry [...]. The Sacrament of Orders alone authorizes those who receive it to speak and act *in persona Christi*."[72] This is not to denigrate the position of the faithful but to avoid the further confusion of roles in the Church. In the same talk, the Pope explained:

> I would like to thank all of the lay people who, by virtue of the power of Baptism, offer the Church their lively support. Precisely because the active witness of lay people is so important, it is equally important not to confuse the special profiles of respective roles.[73]

The specific role of the laity, according to Vatican II, is to preach the Gospel in the marketplace, at home, at work – wherever they find themselves in the world. This highlights the importance in their active role of sharing in the ordained's task of proclaiming the Gospel to all nations.

The priest needs to prepare diligently to preach, but then he must trust the Holy Spirit working through him in the Liturgy of the Word, which is entrusted to his ministry. He needs to be a receptive hearer of the Word and drink deeply from the font of the Scriptures. From the abundance of his heart, he will speak God's message. Grace builds on nature, and homilies need to be prepared through prayerful study and preparation, and then presented in a passionate and loving way that presents Jesus Christ as Lord and Savior of his life. The Congregation for the Clergy encourages priests to be well prepared: "A renewed doctrinal, theological and spiritual proclamation of the Christian message, aimed primarily to enthuse and purify the conscience of the baptized, cannot be achieved through irresponsible or indolent improvisation."[74] The faithful deserve the best the priest can possibly give them in the proclamation of the Good News! As he prepares the homily, he should be asking himself whether it is a word of hope for his people. Abbot Marmion reminds priests that sometimes they will have to exhort and rebuke, but in general they are to remember it is the Good News they are supposed to preach. "In their zeal some priests devote a lot of time to looking at the black side of things [...]. There is no ill-will on their part, it is a kink, a mania which must be corrected."[75] The faithful need to be both encouraged and challenged by the gospel message, a message that should bring life and light.

Shepherding [76]

The priest shares in a unique way the authority of Christ, Who is Head and Shepherd of the Church (*PO* 12 and *PDV* 13). The priest's call is to lovingly shepherd and guide the flock entrusted to him with the same authority he received at ordination by virtue of the sacerdotal character.

St. Paul wrote about the "power" the Lord gave him for the building up of the community (cf. 2 Cor. 10:8 and 13:10). Fr. Jean Galot, S.J., commented on this priestly dimension:

> The priestly character imparts the capacity required to so lead the community in the name of Christ that it will be led more and more by the Lord himself. The character provides the foundation for the empowerment to speak in the name of Christ, to proclaim the Word of God, and to expound with authority the gospel message.[77]

Fr. Galot also wrote:

> The priestly character makes a decisive impact on the structure of the Church. The shepherd guides the community and ensures unity. Because this pastoral mission is ontologically grounded and linked to an indelibly sacramental character, it can be exercised with greater continuity and efficacy. Thanks to the character, the Church enjoys greater structural stability.[78]

Before the priest can shepherd, however, he must be a disciple of the Lord Jesus and His Church. A priest once said: "I love being a priest, because it gives me so much time to be a Christian!" His shepherding is always in the light of obedience to Christ and His Bride. The priest leads from a stance of docility and receptivity to the Truth by being a faithful follower himself.

Shepherding the Church is certainly more than parish administration (although this is no small part of it); he must become a shepherd who "lays down his life for the sheep" (Jn. 10:11). The Good Shepherd is the model of leadership that the priest strives to imitate, for He "did not come to be served but to serve" (Mt. 20:28). Shepherding the flock is about being in relationship. The priest must get to know the parishioners of the parish he serves. Part of the pastoring role of the priest is his presence; the priest-shepherd's presence at the events of people's lives means a great deal to them. His presence is a blessing to them as he visits their home, goes to the hospital, attends an athletic event, or simply stands outside after Mass to greet the parishioners.

He must also be a good steward of the goods of the parish. The good shepherd is not like the hired hand, interested in his own gain, but is always looking to the needs of his flock. Living in union with the Good Shepherd, the priest is able to discern the good for the sake of his people. This docile, discerning posture allows him to pray with the psalmist: "The LORD is my shepherd; there is nothing I lack" (Ps. 23:1).

Healing [79]

The priest also discovers in his identity the call to be "spiritual physician." He bears within himself the authority of Christ the Healer, which was such a large part of His ministry when he walked the earth (cf. Mk. 5:21-43 and 10:46-52). Christ explicitly gave this authority to the Twelve to heal in His name (Mk. 6:7-12, 16:15-18, and Acts 3:1-10). The priest possesses Christ's *exousia* in order to bless, comfort, and heal the sick, lonely, and afraid in his midst. This is not something he can learn but something within him, a capacity which can mature with time and discernment.

The priest is healer *par excellence* in the celebration of the Sacraments of Healing: Reconciliation and the Anointing of the Sick. These are obvious ecclesial moments in which the faith expresses Christ operating through the priest *ex opere operato*. Spiritual healing always flows from these two fonts, and at times even physical healing may follow as well. The power of God working through the sacraments cannot be limited.

Christ is also operative whenever a priest blesses or prays over his people. This is an aspect was perhaps neglected until recent decades. The priest must believe the person before him can and may be healed (physically and always spiritually) by Christ through his prayer over them. This is a powerful realization which must be embraced if the priest is to be Christ's presence in the world – Jesus desires every priest to be a spiritual physician. There should be no shame or confusion when parishioners approach their spiritual father for prayer, whether it is for physical, spiritual, or psychological healing. He is to be a master at the art of praying for his people, which means that he must also become a master at the art of the "discernment of spirits" mentioned in the *Prologue* of this book.[80]

For the priest to be the healer Christ desires him to be, he must first be healed and continually reconciled. The priest is not simply a "wounded healer"; he is to be a "healed wounded healer," turning constantly to the Divine Physician to be mended and made whole. This occurs through open and honest spiritual direction and regular confession of sins. When the priest is in relationship with Christ through ongoing conversion, aware of his own weakness and Christ's strength through him, he will be able to bring great healing into the world.

This principle of communion with Christ is founded on the priest's relationship with Christ and His mission. It encompasses preaching, healing, and shepherding and explains a unique, priestly spirituality involving a receptive relationship with Christ, enabling the priest to then offer Christ to the people. Priestly presence is both a gift and task which seasoned pastors understand and younger priests must learn. A priestly presence, a man who radiates Christ to the world, is strengthened through integrated spirituality. Specifically, Fr. Robert Christian, O.P., comments:

> Therefore, the instrumental functions of presbyters require a permanent "receptivity" to the power of Christ and a permanent capability for serving with those special powers. This essentially distinct *esse* points to some specific difference between priestly spirituality and other forms of spirituality. And even if, *de facto*, because of his assignment, health, or the charism of his community, a particular priest does not engage in the full round of duties normally called "pastoral," he can never lose his ontological identity nor the distinctive life of the Spirit in him that comes with ordination.[81]

All of his actions, not only those performed as the sacramental actions of the Church, are thus priestly actions. Christ's power and authority (*exousia*) are given to him at ordination and come from his very being. Fr. Galot notes:

> The priestly character is the gospel imprinted on his very being [...]. He must carry in his own self the genuine traits of the Savior, and he must let them radiate. [...] The priest is a priest no matter in what endeavor he happens to engage, secular activities included. His priestly being resists cancellation.[82]

In summary, the uniqueness of priestly spirituality is in the renunciation of self completely to Christ, guided both by the permanent receptivity to the power of Christ and the permanent capability for serving the Church with the gifts of preaching, shepherding, and healing. Accordingly, the aim of a constant self-renunciation is to make increasingly evident "I live, no longer I, but Christ lives in me" (Gal. 2:20).

Fifth Principle: Avoidance of Functionalism
Unless the Lord build the house,
they labor in vain who build it.
(Ps. 127:1)

The Congregation for the Clergy continually warns parish priests to "avoid the danger of any form of functionalism. A parish priest is not a functionary fulfilling a role or providing services to those who request them. Rather, he exercises his ministry in an integral way as a man of God [...]" (*PPLP* 22). Functionalism can be understood in two distinct ways. The first stems from the denial of the ontological character and indelible mark given at ordination. Those who embrace this deconstruction of Holy Orders, as seen in the second chapter, believe that the priest is only a priest because he functions as such. In this case, being is doing. Another and more common group of functionalists reject their being in practice because they are simply too busy and do not take time to reflect upon who they are (or Whose) and the reasons behind what they are doing. This kind of functionalism can be called activism, utilitarianism, professionalism, or pragmatism, and it disregards the deep and spiritual nature of the priesthood. Pope Benedict XVI warned a group of newly ordained bishops of the danger of "exaggerated activism" and of the need for balance: "To live in profound union with Christ will help you attain that balance necessary between interior recollection and the necessary effort required by the many occupations of life, avoiding falling into an exaggerated activism."[83] This form of functionalism leads the priest to believe that taking time for prayer, study, and relationships is a waste of time in his overly busy schedule or useless for the parish apostolate.

Supernatural Sensitivity

The mistake both groups of functionalists make is forgetting or denying that the actions of a priest flow from his being conformed to Christ's priesthood. Because he is a priest, he does those things particular to his nature, above all the celebration of the sacraments. The priest who loses the sense of supernatural transcendence and ceases to believe he possesses a sacred character is on the path to ruin. Fr. Dominic Maruca, S.J., notes four factors that have lead to the ruin of many priestly vocations: "(1) an increasing absorption in what were essentially secular activities; (2) sufficient income to assure financial security; (3) a declining interest in traditional sacramental activity; (4) affective involvement"[84] inappropriate to his state in life. Numbers one and three reflect a functional mentality, particularly as explained by Maruca, stating that many

> were no longer happy with sacramental activities that gave scant visible evidence of concrete results. [...] Some began to wonder aloud whether belief in symbolic sacramental efficacy was not merely an anachronistic residue from a past religious era. Such doubts, I think, gradually weakened their bond with the sacramental aspects of priestly ministry."[85]

The priesthood is not simply a job but a way of life, a vocation from God. Without this understanding, the priesthood can be seen as just another profession. Functionalism, activism, or professionalism is the tendency to busy himself to the point of forgetting the very reason he is a priest. The functional role has been stressed in recent years to the detriment of the sacral role. The 2002 Instruction from the Congregation for the Clergy noted: "Internal dangers to the priestly ministry [...] exist: bureaucracy, functionalism, democratization, planning which is more managerial than pastoral." The same document notes the consequences of such an outlook:

> A largely secularized culture which seeks to isolate the priest within his own conceptual

categories and strip him of his fundamental mystical-sacramental dimension, is largely responsible for this phenomenon. From this, several forms of discouragement can derive which lead to isolation, forms of depressive fatalism, and scattered activism (*PPLP* 29).

Falling into this trap of functionalism, the priest loses sight of his true self-identity as a priest of Jesus Christ. Certainly, pastoral charity should be the operative key to everything that the priest does, but he must be aware of overly filling his schedule to the point that this charity eventually becomes a disservice to the people of God and himself. The 1994 *Directory on the Ministry and Life of Priests* reminded priests: "Pastoral charity runs, today especially, the danger of being emptied of its meaning through so-called functionalism" (*DMLP* 44). The Directory also warned priests about losing their sense of identity by "a growing *exterior activism*, submitting [...] to a frenetic and disordered pace" (*DMLP* 40). The danger is that the priest could reduce his self-understanding to what he does, with no real value or reflection given to who he is.

Because a priest's life is centered around the Eucharist and dispensation of the other sacraments, the priest can look back at the end of the day and ask himself how much he has accomplished. Certainly, he has accomplished a great deal on a supernatural level by having celebrated the mysteries of Christ, but this evaluation entails a theological and philosophical understanding of spiritual reality that can be forgotten when too busy. Much of being a priest is not quantifiable. Society today is very utilitarian; if something does not seem useful, it is thought to be less important. Therefore, if the priest does not understand the inestimable value of who he is as a priest, he may fall into the temptation of discouragement or despair (cf. *PPLP* 29). According to Fr. William Sheridan: "Functionalism pervades our culture. There is a tendency to measure things, ideas, and even people by what they do or produce. Our culture values usefulness over essence and the bottom line over the human person."[86]

The active priest with many demands may begin to wonder if what he "does" defines him. The good, hardworking diocesan priest can easily fall into that trap. "Priests," Fr. Aschenbrenner states, "cannot simply be reduced to a list of functions or a litany of priestly activities without paying a costly price."[87] He explains that the "functions" the priest offers the community, even though sacred and sublime, do not confer identity. Secondary functions, such as temporal concerns, meetings, and appointments, as important as they may be, do not define the priest. The priest must resist the temptation to lose his identity in "busy work."[88] Losing sight of his primary sacerdotal mission, he could easily become a kind of social worker or functionary. Archbishop Dolan wrote: "Thus we must again reclaim the superiority of being, and of identity, over doing. A man is a priest before he ministers as one."[89] Pope Benedict XVI said: "To overrate 'doing', obscuring 'being', does not help to recompose the fundamental balance that everyone needs in order to give their own existence a solid foundation and valid goal."[90]

Balance in the life of the priest is a very important factor. The priest must balance the realization of the gift of the sacerdotal character permanently within him regardless of what he does with his service to the people of God by reason of that character. This balance must be sought daily by explicitly recognizing who he is as a ministerial priest. The recognition of his ontological identity is expected to be grounded in years of study and reflection on the nature of the priesthood. One way to maintain balance is to remember constantly that the priestly vocation is about relationship. This relationship is primarily one with God, to continue to grow in knowledge and friendship with Him and serve Him in His people out of love. If the priest ceases to "remain in [His] love" (Jn. 15:9), he runs the risk of doing a lot of things *for* the Lord but not *with* the Lord. Pope John Paul II spoke to the priests of Ireland along these lines: "A constant danger with priests, even zealous priests, is that they become so immersed in the work of the Lord that they neglect the Lord of the work."[91] The *Directory on the Ministry and Life of Priests* emphasizes this truth:

> It is not rare, in fact, to perceive, even in some priests, the influence of an erroneous mentality which reduces the ministerial priesthood to strictly functional aspects. To merely play the role of the priest, carrying out a few services and ensuring completion of various tasks would make up the entire priestly existence. Such a reductive conception of the identity of the ministry of the priest risks pushing their lives towards an emptiness, an emptiness which often comes to be filled by lifestyles not consonant with their very ministry. The priest, who knows how to be the minister of Christ and his

Spouse, will also find in prayer, in study, and in spiritual reading, the strength necessary to overcome these dangers (*DMLP* 40).

Prayerfully Grounded

The priest is to seek balance in the active pastoral life by remaining a man of prayer. By ordination, he has been set apart and consecrated to God. He is to be a man of holiness, without being aloof from his people. Fr. Jean Galot, S.J., notes: "There is, then, no reason to contrast personal holiness with priestly activity. These belong together; they strengthen each other."[92]

Regarding spending time in personal prayer, or as St. Teresa of Avila would quip, "wasting time with God,"[93] the seemingly useless, is of great importance in the life of the priest. Writing of the importance of the priest's prayer life, Blessed Teresa of Calcutta stated:

> Prayer is the food of life of a priest. A priest who does not pray cannot stay close to Christ, he cannot allow Christ to use him as He wants to use him. The fruit of prayer is always [the] deepening of faith, and unless the priest has that deepening of faith, it is very difficult for him to pray. And the fruit of faith is always love. And if a priest does not love, how will he help others to love? And the fruit of love is service – service as Jesus said: "I have come amongst you as one to serve." And the priest is meant to be that one, to come amongst his own, and be the servant of all.[94]

A deep prayer life yields the proper interior strength and depth to secure the mission entrusted to the priest. John Paul II said to a group of priests regarding prayer: "Do not be afraid that time dedicated to the Lord will take anything away from your apostolate. On the contrary, it will be the source of fruitfulness in the ministry."[95] Pope Benedict XVI has been reminding priests of this as well:

> Let us not be consumed with haste, as if time dedicated to Christ in silent prayer were time wasted. On the contrary, it is precisely then that the most wonderful fruits of pastoral service come to birth. There is no need to be discouraged on account of the fact that prayer requires effort, or because of the impression that Jesus remains silent. He is indeed silent, but He is at work. [...]
>
> The faithful expect only one thing from priests: that they be specialists in promoting the encounter between man and God. The priest is not asked to be an expert in economics, construction or politics. He is expected to be an expert in the spiritual life.[96]

The faithful turn to their priest, just as the disciples turned to the Lord and say "teach us to pray" (Lk. 11:1). The priest must become an expert in prayer; if he fails to do this, he has missed the genuine call of the Father to choose the better part (see Lk. 10:42). He thus fails to lead his people into a deeper relationship with God.

The shepherds of the Church are not oblivious of the demands placed on pastors. As these demands increase, so does the need to replenish the dry well at the river of life (see

Rev. 22:1). Attentive to the needs of today's pastors, Pope Benedict XVI, when he was Prefect of the Congregation for the Doctrine of the Faith, wrote:

> In n. 14 the decree [*PO*] speaks of the difficult problem of the interior unity of his life that the priest has to deal with when he is faced with a great number of different tasks; it is a problem which, with the continuing decline in the number of priests, threatens to become ever more the real crisis of priestly existence. A pastor today, who is in charge of three or four parishes, and always on the move from one place to the other, a situation that the missionaries know well, is becoming more the norm for the countries of ancient Christianity. The priest, who must try to guarantee the celebration of the sacraments in the communities, is tormented by administrative duties, is challenged by the complexity of every kind of question, and is aware of the difficulties of persons that he does not even have the time to contact. Torn between the variety of activities, the priest becomes drained and finds fewer opportunities for the recollection, which would give him the new energy and inspiration. Externally stretched and interiorly drained, he loses the joy of his vocation, which in the end he feels to be an unbearable burden. There is nothing left but flight. [...] The foundation is an intimate communion with Christ whose food was to do the will of the Father (John 4:34). It is important that the ontological union with

Christ abide in the conscience and in action: all that I do, I am doing in communion with Him. By doing it, I am with Him. All my activities, no matter how varied and often externally divergent constitute only one vocation: to be together with Christ acting as an instrument in communion with Him.[97]

If the priest is to survive and thrive amidst the complexities of contemporary pastoral activity, he must embrace a contemplative way of living in union with God. In 2006, in a homily to his former Congregation, Pope Benedict XVI said: "silence and contemplation have a purpose: they serve, in the distractions of daily life, to preserve permanent union with God. This is their purpose: that union with God may always be present in our souls and may transform our entire being."[98]

The priest cannot give the faithful what they need if he does not first posses it. *Nemo dat quod non habet.*[99] An intimate relationship in the Heart of the Trinity keeps the priest grounded in the ultimate realities of life. Pope Benedict XVI encourages: "Whoever wants to be a friend of Jesus and become his authentic disciple – be it seminarian, priest, Religious or lay person – must cultivate an intimate friendship with Him in meditation and prayer."[100] The deliberate and continuous effort to safeguard and magnify a keen sense of the supernatural is a practical principle vital to providing a healthier framework for priests today.

Sixth Principle: Ongoing Formation

For this reason, I remind you to stir into flame the gift of God
that you have through the imposition of my hands.
(2 Tim. 1:6)[101]

John Paul II wrote:

Ongoing formation helps the priest to overcome the temptation to reduce his ministry to an activism which becomes an end in itself, to the provision of impersonal services, even if these are spiritual or sacred, or to a business-like function which he carries out for the Church. Only ongoing formation enables the priest to *safeguard with vigilant love the 'mystery' which he bears within his heart for the good of the Church and of mankind* (*PDV* 72).

It is crucial for priests to continue to deepen their understanding of their identity by virtue of ordination. If priests do not "re-cognize" ("to know again") the radical configuration to Christ through the Sacrament of Holy Orders and deepen this knowledge through prayer and study, they risk losing sight of the source and purpose of their ministry. They bear the love of God and the ministry of Christ continued through the Apostles. Study and reflection (*lectio divina*) allow priests to consider who they are and the love that God has for them.

Consecrated Study

Ongoing formation is not a new idea or thought. Instead busy priests in the active apostolate need more frequent reminders of and resources for ongoing formation. In the 6th century Mozarabic Rite of Ordination, the ordination prayer expressly reminds the ordinand his formation and study must continue: "May he also educate himself in his own mind, and make his body chaste. May he carry out his reading in his work, and may he improve his work by reading."[102] Consecrated study keeps priests grounded in their relationship with God (as His beloved sons), with the teachings of the Church (as Her steward), and ultimately their own identity (as priests of Jesus Christ). In 1935 Pope Pius XI wrote:

> Venerable Brethren, it is necessary that the priest, even among the absorbing tasks of his charge, and ever with a view to it, should continue his theological studies with unremitting zeal. The knowledge acquired at the seminary is indeed a sufficient foundation with which to begin; but it must be grasped more thoroughly, and perfected by an ever-increasing knowledge and understanding of the sacred sciences.[103]

Throughout the centuries priests have been encouraged to further their theological learning, and the past few decades have been no exception.[104] The awareness of the dire need is increasing, especially as pastoral duties are increasing.

Regarding ongoing formation of priests, the bishops of the United States wrote: "Following the footsteps of Vatican II's *Presbyterorum Ordinis* and John Paul II's *Pastores Dabo*

Vobis, we can define ongoing formation in this way: It is the continuing integration of priestly identity and functions or service for the sake of mission and communion with Christ and the Church."[105] This integration can only be properly understood by knowing priestly identity and the sacerdotal mission within the life of the Church today. The bishops further explain what they mean by integration:

> For many, the word "integration" may be either vague or seem to reduce spirituality to psychological processes. In the context of ongoing formation, integration is quite specific and spiritual. It signals the movement toward a unity of life that draws together and dynamically relates who we are, what we do, and what we are about (our purpose or mission). As a movement toward a unity of life, the aim of integration is to find the *unum necessarium*, "the one necessary thing," of the Gospel and to live centered in it.[106]

Unity of life, spiritually and psychologically, is crucial for healthy leadership within the Church. Since integration takes time, formation is ongoing: "It takes a while for the psychology to catch up with the ontology."[107] Permanent formation and study serve as a constant aid for the priest.

> There is a reciprocal relationship between spiritual and intellectual formation. The intellectual life nourishes the spiritual life, but the spiritual also opens vistas of understanding, in accordance with the classical adage *credo ut intelligam* ('I believe in order to know') (*PPF* 136).[108]

Theology in general, particularly theology that deepens the understanding of the priestly vocation within the life of the Church, is a high priority for ongoing formation of the priest. At an international symposium of bishops and priests sponsored by the Congregation for the Clergy, the concluding message stated:

> In order that the priest might be 'the salt and leaven' in actual social and cultural circumstances, we recommend an ongoing profound awareness regarding priestly identity. It is the clarity and the continual understanding of a priest's proper identity that establishes equilibrium in his life and the fruitfulness of the pastoral ministry he assumes.[109]

The PPF stresses the

> necessity of helping seminarians commit themselves wholeheartedly to ongoing formation after ordination. The process and the journey of the ongoing formation of priests is both necessary and lifelong. Its purpose is not only the spiritual growth of the priest himself but also the continued effectiveness of his mission and ministry (*PPF* 368).

At the same time, ongoing formation is broader than just theology. It should also include the study of, or at least an awareness of, the secular sciences and cultural factors of the day to be more prepared to minister to the people. "There is a need, then, to be aware of, and to understand, the world in which we live [...]" (*Gaudium et Spes* 4).[110] This document of Vatican II further stressed that priests "should study carefully to equip themselves to play their part in entering into dialogue with the world and with people of every persuasion" (*GS* 43). Priests and theologians should pursue knowledge in the fields of science, philosophy, history, psychology, sociology, literature, and the arts, to be able to address people in the modern world and thus show them the relevance of the Gospel (cf. *GS* 62).[111]

Unfortunately there is often a void and diminishing interest in (or time for) continuing education once ordained. As Fr. James Gill, S.J., M.D., wrote:

> To meet this same need as a priest, he will have to take the initiative to regularly attend gatherings of priests, participate in retreats and workshops, and read publications designed to help priests like himself maintain their pastoral skills and fulfill their role in ministry.[112]

Ongoing formation is crucial for the health of the priest; this genuine need must be met, or the priest will suffer.

Time can always be found to read, study, and contemplate, even in the busiest of parishes, if ongoing formation is made a priority. Free-time, offers a temptation for priests to escape, specifically with the use of the television and the computer or internet, when true rest and recreation is required. Granted, priests need and deserve a break, but they should limit "prolonged and unbalanced use of *mass media*,"[113] particularly when it does not edify or re-create and renew their priestly spirit.[114] While they certainly have their place as a form of entertainment, studies show that TV and internet use does not truly relax the mind and heart. The priest must safeguard his priestly identity from negative, secular influences that could harm his vocation. In 2004 Pope John Paul II said: "People grow or diminish in moral stature by the words which they speak and the messages which they choose to hear. Consequently, wisdom and discernment in the use of the media are particularly called for [...]."[115]

Temptations often arise in moments of idleness: temptations against chastity and charity, temptations to isolation and self-pity. If the priest has formed healthy habits of relaxing and fostering his priestly heart, moments of solitude will not be inordinately filled with unhealthy forms of escapism. The Pontifical Council for Social Communication encourages:

> As an antidote to time-wasting, sometimes even alienating indulgence in superficial media programmes, the [seminarian/priest] should be guided to the love and practice of reading, study, silence and meditation. [...] This will serve to remedy the isolation and self-absorption caused by the unidirectional communication of the *mass media*, and will revive the authentic and absolute value proper to the Christian profession and the priestly ministry, particularly those of obedience and evangelical poverty, which the materialist and consumerist vision of human existence offered by the instruments of social communication very often ignores.[116]

Three years later the same Pontifical Council issued a letter warning the faithful, including priests and consecrated, to be "discriminating consumers of media," especially in light of the assault of the entertainment which devalues human sexuality and the virtue of modesty and chastity.[117] The discipline of ongoing formation can be helpful for the priest to become more discriminating in his entertainment choices. He knows how to use his time well and fill it with healthy alternatives. Aside from study, healthy habits include spending time in priestly fraternity, developing relationships with friends and family, physical exercise, constructive hobbies, and pleasure reading. These, in moderation, are never a waste of time; they renew the heart and elevate the mind. "[S]tudy is not time lost from work; it is time spent so that one may know how – and why – to work."[118]

The first step in ongoing formation is to recognize it as a genuine need. It is not difficult to imagine the busy pastor who has not picked up a theological text in over a decade. Would not his spiritual life be better and his homilies deeper if he were to enter into a period of study everyday, even if for fifteen minutes? A realistic goal for a priest is to engage in some form of spiritual reading daily: scriptural, theological, hagiographical, inspirational, catechetical, or classical. Entering into this reading by opening his heart to the Spirit of the Living God (*lectio divina*), he will find nourishment he would not have previously imagined.

Accountability

Daily study is important, but so are programs of formation for the spiritual life and the apostolate. Seminars and annual retreats are very often lost in the busy schedule of today's pastors. "Ongoing formation is a right-duty of the priest and imparting it is a right-duty of the Church" (*DMLP* 72). Accountability of priests to their bishops as to the exact nature, duration, and programs they choose is needed now more than ever. This serves not as a punishment but as a form of accountability so this need is met. The burden falls upon the priest himself, first and foremost, but the local ordinary is obligated to ensure that his priests are receiving good and balanced continuing education. Bishops must verify that their priests have an annual retreat, are involved in continuous education, and be aware of the programs they are attending (cf. *DMLP* 88). Then Bishop, now Archbishop, Wuerl wrote:

> The individual priest has the obvious, primary responsibility for his growth and conversion to the Lord. At the same time, the diocesan bishop is to exercise the greatest care in the progressive formation of the presbyterate. [...] In addition, it is under his direction that the diocese provides resources and develops clear policies and expectations for the ongoing formation of priests.[119]

Msgr. Kelly similarly noted that a "lack of oversight begets a lack of discipline, and of unity, for which Church authorities alone are responsible. [...] And the only way to restore oversight to its proper place in the Church is to do it."[120] Most professions require hours of annual course work to stay current. Although priests are not professionals in the secular sense, they still need to deepen their competency in areas essential to pastoral ministry. The spiritual ministry of priests is the most important work in the world. If this is so, the importance for them to stay current in their field of expertise – theology and the care of souls – is even greater. For example, priests could be required to participate in specific ongoing formation to maintain priestly faculties in a particular diocese. Cardinal Bevilacqua noted: "Every profession requires a constant updating on the part of its participants, and we must demand no less of those who are ordained to the priesthood."[121] While many possibilities exist, effective continuing education programs for priests are fundamental to the relevancy and currency of their personal growth processes. Bishops, as spiritual fathers of their priests, need to take a more active role in the care of their pastors. If the priests are fed, the people will be fed. The Congregation for the Clergy wrote of the need for bishops to provide this ongoing formation for their priests:

> [B]ishops, as fathers and pastors, are urged to offer their priests always greater opportunities to reflect on their priestly identity, making use of the means that are most effective to achieve this end: retreats, days of recollection and fraternal fellowship, conferences. Additionally, they should knowingly encourage respect which comes from a concerned familiarity with their own priests. With particular solicitude, it is recommended that they adequately present to all their priests all documents either of the Pontiff or the Dicasteries of the Holy See which pertain to the ministry and life of priests. Those who are chosen as presenters of these documents should be chosen for their preparation and proven orthodoxy.[122]

Bearing Abundant Fruit

Regular study and continual growth in faith keeps the priest grounded in the truth of the Gospel and teachings of the Church. Pope John Paul II wrote: "Ongoing formation helps the priest to be and act as a priest in the spirit and style of Jesus the Good Shepherd" (*PDV* 73). Through his study and prayer he will "*safeguard and develop his awareness of the total and marvelous truth of his being*: he is a minister of Christ and steward of the mysteries of God (cf. 1 Cor. 4:1)" (*PDV* 73, emphasis added). Reflecting regularly upon these realities allows the priest to be grateful for the sublime mysteries entrusted to him and are within him. As Fr. Mark O'Keefe, O.S.B., observes: "if we took the time to ponder the indelible nature of the call to the priesthood, we would find at least three dispositions growing up within us: gratitude, commitment, and conversion."[123]

Proper knowledge through study helps the priest love God, neighbor, and self, allowing him to appreciate his own vocation as a gift. St. Thomas Aquinas wrote of the importance of knowledge: "For we do not love anything unless we apprehend it by a mental conception."[124] Following this thought, Fr. Robert Christian, O.P., wrote: "The study of divine truth, then, naturally leads one to pray to his Beloved, while love of one's beloved drives one to want to know his truth more assiduously."[125] *Contemplata aliis tradere.*[126] Study leads to the possibility of greater loving. Therefore knowledge, specifically knowledge resulting from ongoing formation, assists the priest in correctly ordering his affection and forming a true interior unity that allows Christ the High

Priest to transform the actions of his day.[127] The documents calling priests to ongoing formation are ample; now the initiative and response of both priests and bishops is needed to bring its implementation to fruition.

As the priest reflects upon Christ the Priest and grows in a deeper love for Him, he will grow in understanding of how he shares in that same priesthood. By virtue of ordination, the priest is called to lead a life of holiness, not just for the sake of his own soul but for the sake of the souls of the faithful for whom he stands *in persona Christi capitis*.[128] The more the priest lives a life of holiness, the more he is filled with an inner peace, a deep love for God, and a joy that is contagious. Because of his growth in knowledge, the priest is able better to assimilate who he is and act upon it – *agere sequitur esse*. The proper understanding of the ministerial priesthood is of utmost importance for priests so they may respond to the gift within them.

Notes

1 "Priests, Be What You Are and Have the Courage of Fidelity!: Address to the Clergy and Male Religious in Palermo," 20 November 1982, *ORE* (6 December 1982), 12.

2 Ibid, 9.

3 "You Are Servants of the People of God: Address to Priests and Men Religious in Mexico," 27 January 1979, *ORE* (12 February 1979), 4.

4 Timothy Costello, S.M., *Forming a Priestly Identity: Anthropology of Priestly Formation in the Documents of the VIII Synod of Bishops and the Apostolic Exhortation* Pastores Dabo Vobis (Roma: Editrice Pontificia Università Gregoriana, 2002), 237 and 214.

5 Benedict XVI, "Immerse Yourselves in the Love of the Saviour," 2.

6 *The Meaning of Christian Priesthood*, trans. Paedar MacSeumais, S.J. (Westminster, Maryland: Christian Classics, 1989), 109.

7 *Quickening the Fire in Our Midst: The Challenge of Diocesan Priestly Spirituality* (Chicago: Loyola Press, 2002), 68-81.

8 Ibid., 69.

9 Ibid., 74. Aschenbrenner writes of the ontological character of the priesthood earlier in *Quickening the Fire in Our Midst* and emphasizes the importance of understanding it for the proper formation of a priestly identity (ibid., cf. 32-34, found in the chapter entitled "Identity and Territory").

10 Ibid., 75.

11 Timothy M. Dolan, "The Formation of Candidates for the Ministry of the New Evangelization," *Seminary Journal* 8.2 (Autumn 2002): 18.

12 Aschenbrenner, *Quickening the Fire in Our Midst*, 78-79.

13 Ibid., 70. As Aschenbrenner notes, a factor that may have significant consequences on a priest's perception of the sacramental character and of its permanency is the "postmodern" mentality. Postmodern thought is influencing much of our society today and consequently affecting people's framing of spiritual realities, such as the understanding of permanent commitments. Fr. Donald Cozzens has noted that Postmodernism: "announces not only the loss of a unifying worldview that previously gave meaning and purpose to the sacrifices inherent to the priesthood and religious life, but it challenges the validity of belief systems themselves. If the Enlightenment led to scientism and secularism, postmodernism provokes a radical relativism and the collapse of the transcendent" (*Sacred Silence: Denial and the Crisis in the Church* [Collegeville: Liturgical Press, 2002], 87). Cf. also, Donald L. Gelpi, *Varieties of Transcendental Experience: A Study in Constructive Postmodernism* (Collegeville: Liturgical Press, 2000), 339 and

Thomas Guarino, "Postmodernity and Five Fundamental Theological Issues," *Theological Studies* 57 (December 1996): 654-689.

14 Ibid., 81. "Whatever deceptively interferes with his priestly call, whether a mood of happy feelings or a burdensome feeling of boredom and failure, is now interpreted as the temptation of an unholy spirit. Following the guidance of God's Spirit in resisting the deceptive insinuations of the evil spirit becomes very practical and concrete. Insightful courage and trust in God's promise of a faithful priestly call become the issue at hand. Now the young priest who falls in love presumes that this is not a call away from his priestly commitment. Rather, the issue is what kind of relationship, if any, he is to welcome with this woman. The priest who is bored and losing the glow of his priestly commitment presumes he is not being called away from priestly ministry but must rather investigate means to renew himself and rekindle the fire of his permanent priestly commitment" (ibid., 80).

15 Executive Director of the USCCB Secretariat of Clergy, Consecrated Life and Vocations.

16 "Sociological and Cultural Issues Affecting Priestly Vocations," *The Priest*, November 2006, 12.

17 "Confront the Crisis in Vocations Prayerfully and Practically – *Ad limina Apostolorum*: Bishops' Conference of France – 2," 19. To the same group, he noted that the "social environment [is] marked by widespread relativism of 'values' broadcast by the media, the trivialization of sexuality and scandals connected with it, demand that special be paid to the human, emotional and moral formation of candidates" (ibid., 5).

18 "Knowing the Joy of Serving: Interview with Vatican Radio and German Television Networks," *ORE*, 30 August 2006, 5.

19 The four identities of the priesthood as identified by the Institute for Priestly Formation are Chaste Spouse, Spiritual Father, Spiritual Physician, and Good Shepherd. Each of these identities was the theme of a symposium, beginning in 2001 and published in 2008. Regarding the topic of Chaste Spouse, see the first volume of the series: *Chaste Celibacy: Living Christ's own Spousal Love*, proceedings of the *First Annual Symposium on the Spirituality and Identity of the Diocesan Priest*. Particularly insightful is Bishop Allen Vigneron's presentation entitled "Renewed Celibate Living for Heralds of the New Evangelization," 13-27.

20 Aschenbrenner, *Quickening the Fire in Our Midst*, 124.

21 Cf. Federico Suarez, *About Being a Priest* (Princeton, New Jersey: Scepter, 1996), 161. This assertion is also contained in other sources, such as Sara Butler, "The Priest as Sacrament of Christ the Bridegroom," *Worship* 66.6 (Nov. 1992): 512-513; Andrew R. Baker, "Here Comes the Groom: The

Priest as Bridegroom of the Church," *Lay Witness*, May/June 2003, 24-25; Genevieve S. Kineke, "The Nuptial Meaning of the Priesthood: Why the Priesthood is for Men," *Lay Witness*, May/June 2003, 40-41.

22 *Priestly Identity: A Study in the Theology of Priesthood*, 86 (cf. also, *DMLP* 13).

23 *Theology of the Body* (Boston: Daughters of St. Paul, 1997), 277. A good summary article for priests to read regarding Theology of the Body is by Fr. John Balluff, "The Theology of the Body and Troubling Attractions," *The Priest*, September 2006, 40-47.

24 See the published proceedings by the Institute for Priestly Formation: *Spiritual Fatherhood: Living Christ's Own Revelation of the Father* (Omaha, 2003).

25 Cf. *LG* 21, 28; *PO* 9, 16, 19.

26 Evans, "*In Persona Christi* – the Key to Priestly Identity," 123.

27 "The Paternal Order of Priests," *Lay Witness*, May/June 2003, 8. Dr. Hahn continues: "Like any father, priests must take responsibility, [...] provide for, teach them, exhort them, discipline them, guide them, correct them, and forgive them. [...] For priesthood, like my fatherhood, is not a job; it's not an administrative role. It's a vocation from God. There's a big difference between a job and a vocation, and it manifest itself in countless ways" (ibid., 7-8).

28 *Priests for the Third Millennium*, 70.

29 "Raising Up Priests for the New Millennium," *Lay Witness*, May/June 2003, 5.

30 "Immerse Yourselves in the Love of the Saviour," 20.

31 David N. Power, *Ministers of Christ and His Church: The Theology of the Priesthood*, 176.

32 Cf. *ST* III, q. 64, a. 6.

33 "Life and Ministry of Priests," in *Priesthood: A Greater Love*, 122.

34 *Priesthood: A Re-examination of the Roman Catholic Theology of the Presbyterate*, 148

35 John Paul II, *Priesthood in the Third Millennium: Addresses of Pope John Paul II, 1993*, ed. James P. Socias (Princeton: Scepter Publishers, 1994), 65.

36 *Ecclesia de Eucharistia*, 31. Worried about functionalism in the life of his priests, Pope John Paul II continued: "Priests are engaged in a wide variety of pastoral activities. If we also consider the social and cultural conditions of the modern world it is easy to understand how priests face the very real *risk of losing their focus* amid such a great number of different tasks. The Second Vatican Council saw in pastoral charity the bond which gives unity to the priest's life and work. This, the Council adds, 'flows mainly from the Eucharistic Sacrifice, which is therefore the centre and root of the whole priestly life' [*PO* 14]" (cf. also *CIC* 276 § 2.2).

37 *Christ the Ideal of the Priest*, 259 [227]. Marmion focuses on the priest's intimate union with Christ and, therefore, with His Mystical Body, the Church, as he prays and intercedes for Her needs *in nomine Ecclesiae*. "The whole life of love which is the priest's should be sustained by a very lively faith in this wondrous unity in Christ. When we celebrate our Mass we should remember that we are offering the sacrifice in the bosom of this tremendous unity which is the Church, and thus we are praying in her name" (*Christ the Ideal of the Priest*, 178 [156]). Dom Marmion wrote in his spiritual journal in 1921: "Every day at Mass I think of all of those who are in trouble or affliction and I ask Christ to pray through my lips for all those miseries; in this way the priest is truly *os totius Ecclesiae*" (*Christ the Ideal of the Priest*, 375 [332]). In a very real way, the priest is the voice of the whole Church.

38 *General Instruction of the Roman Missal*: Third Typical Edition (Washington, D.C.: USCCB, 2003) 114. If the priest does not concelebrate, it is assumed that he is in the sanctuary in choir vesture as the appropriate place for the ordained at the Liturgy; they are not to attend *in modo laico* (cf. *GIRM* 114).

39 "*Sacramentum Unitatis – Unitas Sacramenti*: Concelebration for the Fullness of the Eucharist" (S.T.L. diss., Pontifical Athenaeum of Saint Anselm (Rome), 1998), 54, 71. Similarly, Bishop Aquila of Fargo, in his *tesina* at Rome's *Sant' Anselmo*, wrote: "The ministerial priest in the daily celebration of the Eucharist, and only when he presides or concelebrates, exercises most fully the unity of the actions *in persona Christi* and *in persona Ecclesiae*" (Aquila, 133).

40 Balthasar, *The Christian State of Life*, 306.

41 Kasper, "Ministry in the Church: Taking Issue with Edward Schillebeeckx," 189.

42 Suarez, *About Being a Priest* (Princeton, New Jersey: Scepter, 1996), 11.

43 Macquarrie, *A Guide to the Sacraments*, 185. "The effects of Ordination also show that a priest has a special obligation of tending to perfection" (Garrigou-Lagrange, *The Priest in Union with Christ*, 53; cf. also *ST*, q. 184, a. 7 and 8).

44 *The Priest and the Third Christian Millennium: Teacher of the word, Minister of the Sacraments, and Leader of the Community* (Washington, D.C.: USCC, 1999), 40. cf. 10; cf. *ST* Suppl., q. 34, a. 1 and q. 37, a. 1.

45 Galot, *The Theology of the Priesthood*, 207.

46 USCCB, *The Basic Plan for the Ongoing Formation of Priests* (Washington, D.C.: USCCB, 2001), 10.

47 A professor from the *Urbaniana* wrote: "the 'mission' originates from

the participation in the ontological reality of Christ. The mission encompasses the whole life of the priest since it springs from his consecration. The priestly ministry is not a temporal or circumstantial function, but a definitive election." (Juan Esquerda Bifet, "Missionary Spirit or Functionalism," in *Priesthood: A Greater Love – International Symposium on the Thirtieth Anniversary of the Promulgation of the Conciliar Decree Presbyterorum Ordinis*, 28 October 1995 [Philadelphia: Archdiocese of Philadelphia, 1997], 111).

48 *Christ the Ideal of the Priest*, 113 [99]. As a good Benedictine, Abbot Marmion would have had the words of his founder in mind: "keep death ever before you" (*memento mori – Rule of St. Benedict*, chap. 4), regarding the soul of the priest remaining in the state of grace. He wrote that "judgment is more to be feared by the priest than any other on account of the importance of his sacred functions and his responsibilities: more will be required of those to whom more has been given" (*Christ the Ideal of the Priest*, 107 [93]). The priest must strive to remain in the state of grace for the sake of his own soul: "If it should befall a minister of Christ to celebrate the holy mysteries with a conscience gravely burdened, would he have the right to count himself among the friends of Jesus? He would be committing a sacrilege. [...] I know, and it is an article of our faith, that there is pardon for every sin, but the experience of souls teaches us that this insult to the Son of God causes a terrible blindness. What will be the fate of such a soul if death befalls it unexpectedly? Before we celebrate, let us reflect that it will be for us as it was for those witnesses at the foot of the Cross: each one will receive grace or be hardened in sin according to his dispositions" (*Christ the Ideal of the Priest*, 227 [199]; cf. 111 [97], regarding the eternal punishment of an unfaithful priest).

49 Hacker wrote: "Now the configuration of the priest to Christ is based on a mission which [...] confers a particular being-as-such, an ontological reality; this configuration effects a genuine representation of the Saviour and implies that the ministers' sharing in the priesthood of Christ differs from the common priesthood of all the faithful. [...] In other words, the priest does not bring about the holy mysteries because he is presiding over the community or the Eucharistic celebration; on the contrary, it is because he is by the sacrament of Order, configured to the eternal high priest that he does represent as an instrument, Christ the priest, in the representation of Christ's sacrifice" ("The Priesthood and the Eucharist Today," in *Priesthood and Celibacy*, 337-338).

50 The footnote here cites the following Vatican II texts: *SC* 33; *LG* 10, 28, 37; *PO* 2, 6, 12. Also cited is St. Thomas Aquinas, *ST* III, q. 22, a. 4. Cf. also *ST* III, q. 64, a. 8, *ad* 2 and *ST* Suppl., q. 37, a. 4, *ad* 2. Henri de Lubac noted: "the faithful can not confer or delegate a power which is not theirs" (*The Splendor of the Church*, trans. Michael Mason [Glen Rock, New Jersey: Paulist Press, 1956], 82).

51 Sara Butler, "Priestly Identity: 'Sacrament' of Christ the Head" *Worship* 70.4 (July 1996): 306. *In persona Ecclesiae* is to be interpreted in the way it is explained by the CDF in *Inter Insigniores* (cf. *Inter Insigniores: Declaration Regarding the Question of the Admission of Women to Ministerial Priesthood* (1976), in *From "Inter Insigniores" to "Ordinatio Sacerdotalis": Documents and Commentaries* [Washington, D.C.: USCC, 1998], 47).

52 *In Persona Christi: Reflections on Priestly Identity and Holiness*, 17-18.

53 "The Liturgy of the Hours as Prayer of the Church," in *The Church at Prayer*, vol. 4, *The Liturgy and Time*, ed. A. G. Martimort (Collegeville: Liturgical Press, 1986), 185.

54 *General Instruction of the Liturgy of the Hours*, 28: LOH, 1, 37. The priest, following the example of the bishop, should always pray the Divine Office *in nomine Ecclesiae* (cf. ibid.). Marmion wrote: "The Hours are *Opus Dei*. To say them well is a work much more excellent than many others" (*Christ the Ideal of the Priest*, 267 [234-235]).

55 Cf. ibid., 29: *LOH*, 1, 38. This paragraph states that it is an obligation for priests to "recite the full sequence of the Hours each day, as far as possible at the appropriate times." It continues by explaining each of the five "Hours" of the Divine Office the priest is bound to pray (cf. also *CIC* 276 § 2.3).

56 The footnote which follows the last sentence of the quote references Blessed Columba Marmion, *Christ the Ideal of the Priest*, Chapter 14. "By the very fact that she imposes on us the obligation of the Office, the Church shows us the importance she attaches to it: she obliges *sub gravi* to discharge this duty every day; we are not free except in specified cases, to dispense ourselves from this task. We are bound to devote the necessary time to it. And certainly time is not lost. The most efficacious prayer for the salvation of souls is our breviary" (*Christ the Ideal of the Priest*, 271 [238]).

57 Timothy M. Dolan, "The Divine Office Our Duty: The Priesthood's Renewal Won't Occur Until We Pray the Office Daily," *The Priest*, December 2006, 29. The Archbishop writes of the comfort he finds in the psalms of the Office: "In these troubled days in the life of the Church, I find balm in the psalms of the *Office*" (ibid.).

58 "Rouse Labourers! Enkindle in Them Enthusiasm and Joy for the Gospel: Address to Priests and Deacons in Freising," *ORE*, 20 September, 2006, 13.

59 *Christ the Ideal of the Priest*, 259-260 [228].

60 Ibid., 260-261 [228-229].

61 Ibid., 262 [230].

62 Suarez, *About Being a Priest*, 8. The late Cardinal John O'Connor reminded his priests: "The man who is 'always a priest' has no enduring

identity problems. He knows not only who, but what he is. Nor does he ever try to conceal what he is. He is a priest" (*Always a Priest, Always Present: A Pastoral Letter to the Priests of the Archdiocese of New York* [New York: privately printed, 1989], 4-5).

63 McGovern, *Priestly Identity*, 92.

64 Ibid., 93.

65 When this directory was published, a *dubium* was raised seeking clarification as to the weight of this particular statement. The response stated that the directory's norm is not merely an encouragement but is "juridically binding" according to a seven-point clarification issued by the Pontifical Council of Legislative Texts in November of 1995 (cf. also, *CIC* 284).

66 Over the course of time, the "art" of knowing when wearing the collar is not essential will be developed. Pastors need to be patient with associates who are learning this balance. While on the golf course, at the beach, on the lake, in the woods, and moments of rest and recreation with priests and family – these are times in which the ordained need not be scrupulous about wearing the collar.

67 Rossetti, *The Joy of the Priesthood*, 50-51.

68 "If ever a priest understood the depths of the significance of the Passion and death of Jesus and the immensity of the divine mercy, it was St. Paul. [...] *Vivo ego iam non ego, vivit vero in me Christus* (Gal.2:20). Christ is in me; you see me act, but this zeal, these words are not from me; they are from Christ, Who inspires my whole life, because I have renounced all that I am in order to be completely His minister" (Marmion, *Christ the Ideal of the Priest*, 67 [58]).

69 Dillenschneider, *Dogmatic Foundations of Our Priestly Spirituality*, vol. 1, *Christ the One Priest and We His Priests*, 146, 148-149. The Church mandates that only ordained ministers preach at the liturgy. The *Code of Canon Law* states: "The most important form of preaching is the homily, which is part of the liturgy itself, and is reserved to a priest or deacon" (*CIC* 767).

70 Aschenbrenner, *Quickening the Fire in Our Midst*, 47.

71 This has subsequently been reaffirmed in the 2004 *Instruction* from the Congregation for Divine Worship and the Discipline of the Sacraments, *Redemptionis Sacramentum* (Vatican City: Libreria Editrice Vaticana, 2004), 64-66.

72 "Papal Discourse to the German Bishops on the Occasion of the Visit '*Ad Limina Apostolorum*,'" *ORE*, 29 November 2006, 5. Elsewhere he stated: "the homily is not a discursive interruption in the Liturgy but part of the sacramental event" ("The Discourse of Pope Benedict XVI to the Bishops of Switzerland," *ORE*, 22 November 2006, 10).

73 Ibid.

74 "The Priest: Teacher of the Word, Minister of the Sacraments, Leader of the Community," *Origins*, 9 September 1999, 203.

75 *Christ the Ideal of the Priest*, 173.

76 See the published proceedings by the Institute for Priestly Formation: *Good Shepherd: Living Christ's Own Pastoral Authority* (Omaha, 2006).

77 Galot, *The Theology of the Priesthood*, 208-209.

78 Galot, *The Theology of the Priesthood*, 210.

79 See the published proceedings by the Institute for Priestly Formation: *Spiritual Physician: Living Christ's Own Mission of Healing* (Omaha, 2002).

80 St. Ignatius of Loyola coined this phrase in his *Spiritual Exercises* and offers specific "rules" for discernment (cf. numbers 313-327) which are extraordinarily helpful for the spiritual physician. The Institute for Priestly Formation offers specific insights into the Ignatian methods.

81 "Priestly Spirituality," in *Compendium of Spirituality*, vol. II, ed. Emetrio De Cea, O.P., trans. Jordan Aumann, O.P. (New York: Alba House, 1996),49.

82 *The Theology of the Priesthood*, 207 and 211.

83 "Papal Advice to New Bishops: Pray," 21 September 2006, *Zenit.org* (downloaded on 26 September 2006).

84 "History: School of Humility and Source of Hope: Common Factors in the Lives of Priests Who Left and Those Who Stayed," *The Priest*, May 1994, 34.

85 Ibid., 34-35 (cf. also, *DMLP* 44).

86 William P. Sheridan, "Functionalism Undermining Priesthood," *Human Development* 20, no. 3 (1999): 12. "These values have found their way into almost every facet of modern life. The fields of education, medicine, and technology grapple with functionalism every day. The church too struggles with functionalism as it tries to place mission above money and ministry above technical efficiency. The priesthood is particularly susceptible to functionalism" (ibid.).

87 *Quickening the Fire in Our Midst*, 27.

88 Cf. Segundo Galilea, *Temptation and Discernment*, trans. Stephen-Joseph Ross, O.C.D. (Washington, D.C.: ICS Publications, 1996), 20-45. This section of Galilea's book is entitled "The Demons of Ministry." "The demon of activism is not the same as being very active or a hard worker, or having many jobs and various ministries. Being active as a minister is not falling into 'activism' as a temptation. Activism comes about insofar as it increases the distance and inconsistency between what ministers do and say, between who they are and how they live as Christians. In the human condition we do accept

as normal some incompatibility between 'being' and 'doing.' In the case of activism, though, the incongruity is intensified and tends to grow and not to diminish (as would be ideal in the Christian process). Activism has many expressions. One of them is lack of renewal in the minister's personal life. In a systematic way, prayer is inadequate and poor. There are no prolonged periods of solitude and retreat. The minister does not cultivate study and seldom reads. One does not set aside time to rest sufficiently and recover. Similarly, one has an overload of work and multiple activities, and has packed the appointment book. Activists give the impression that a large volume of exterior work is necessary for their lifestyle. Excessive activity or neglect of renewal creates a vicious cycle. The increased activity makes it increasingly difficult to take measures for interior renewal that lead to growth in 'being.' On the other hand, the increasing incapacity for renewing oneself tends to be compensated for and distinguished by surrendering to uncontrollable activity. In the end, activism is the excuse for 'escapism.' Activism also expresses itself in one of the most radical distortions in ministry: putting one's entire soul into the means of organizing and doing the action of ministry, while at the same time forgetting that it is God who is at its source. The Lord is the one who organizes and accomplishes all things. Activist ministers transform themselves into professionals who multiply initiatives – all of them usually good" (ibid., 25).

89 "The Formation of Candidates for the Ministry of the New Evangelization," 18.

90 "Investigate and Foster the Perennial Value of the Truth," *ORE*, 1 November 2006, 3.

91 "What People Expect of You is Fidelity to the Priesthood: Address to Priests, Missionaries, Religious Brothers and Sisters at Maynooth," 1 October 1979, *ORE*, 15 October 1979, 4. The *DLMP* (71) states: "priests must avoid any dualism between spirituality and ministry, for it is the origin of some profound crises."

92 *Theology of the Priesthood*, 207.

93 Cf. Teresa of Àvila. *The Book of Her Life*, in *The Collected Works of St. Teresa of Àvila*, vol. 1, trans. and ed. Kieran Kavanough, O.C.D. and Otilio Rodriguez, O.C.D. (Washington, D.C.: ICS Publishers, 1987), 96; *The Way of Perfection*, trans. and ed. Kieran Kavanough, O.C.D. (Washington, D.C.: ICS Publishers, 2000), 252.

94 *Testament, Constitutions, and Directory of the Missionaries of Charity Fathers* (Mexico City: privately printed, 1994), 78.

95 John Paul II, "You are Servants of the People of God: Address to Priests and Men Religious in Mexico," 4.

96 Benedict XVI, "Immerse Yourselves in the Love of the Saviour," 4. Cf. James Keating, "The Contemplative Pastor," The Priest (June, 2007), 40-48.

97 "Life and Ministry of Priests," in *Priesthood: A Greater Love – International Symposium on the Thirtieth Anniversary of the Promulgation of the Conciliar Decree Presbyterorum Ordinis*, 28 October 1995, 126. As Pope, Benedict XVI is evidently aware of the many difficulties and duties that are required and expected of priests today. He knows "the burdens have increased. To be looking after two, three, or four parishes at the same time, in addition to all the new tasks that have emerged, can lead to discouragement" ("Rouse Labourers! Enkindle in Them Enthusiasm and Joy for the Gospel: Address to Priests and Deacons in Freising," 12).

98 "Fostering 'Obedience to the Truth,'" *ORE*, 18 October 2006, 4.

99 St. Augustine wrote: *Dare nemo possit quod non habet* (*De Baptismo Contra Donatistas* 5, 20, 28: *PL* 43, 190: trans. NPNF 1, 4). This phrase is commonly cited: "you cannot give what you do not have."

100 "Searching for Truth, Building the Spiritual Life," *ORE*, 1 November 2006, 2.

101 Chapter Six of *Pastores Dabo Vobis*, regarding the ongoing formation of priests, begins with these same words of Paul to Timothy (2 Tim. 1:6).

102 Bradshaw, *Ordination Rites of the Ancient Churches of East and West*, 234. Then Cardinal Ratzinger, now Pope Benedict XVI, wrote: "The will without knowledge is blind and so orthopraxis, without knowledge, is blind and leads to the abyss. [...] The Truth is concrete. Knowledge and action are closely united, as are faith and life" ("Eucharist, Communion and Solidarity," *ORE*, 13 Nov. 2002, 6).

103 *Ad Catholici Sacerdotii: Encyclical Letter on the Catholic Priesthood*, 20 December 1935, 58: *AAS* 28 (1936): trans. *The Papal Encyclicals 1903-1939*, vol. 3, ed. Claudia Carlen, I.H.M. [New York: Consortium, 1981], 34).

104 Cf., *CIC* 279; *PDV* 70-81; *DMLP* 69-97; USCCB, *The Basic Plan for the Ongoing Formation of Priests*; *PPLP* 15-17. Regarding this last *Instruction* of 2002, diverse aspects of the sacramental character are mentioned over twenty times. The Congregation for Clergy has once again emphasized the important aspect of being grounded in the mystery of their priestly identity through a life of prayer and study of the Church's teaching.

105 USCCB, *The Basic Plan for the Ongoing Formation of Priests*, I, C.

106 Ibid.

107 David L. Toups, "Ongoing Formation of a Young Priest," *Touchstone: Newsletter of the NFPC* (Fall 2001): 10. McGovern writes: "It is fairly clear that where the priestly life is concerned there is a close interaction between theology and psychology. [...] To act fully *in persona Christi* requires a

coherent, ascetical, and psychological union with Him whom he is making present to others" (McGovern, *Priestly Identity*, 69 and 81).

108 As St. Augustine wrote: "Therefore, understand, in order to believe; believe, in order to understand: *Ergo intellege ut credas, crede ut intellegas*" (*Sermo* 43, 9: *PL* 38, 258).

109 "International Symposium: Concluding Message to all Priests in the World," in *Priesthood: A Greater Love – International Symposium on the Thirtieth Anniversary of the Promulgation of the Conciliar Decree Presbyterorum Ordinis*, 28 October 1995 (Philadelphia: Archdiocese of Philadelphia, 1997), 337.

110 Pope John Paul II wrote: "The intellectual dimension of formation likewise needs to be continually fostered through the priest's entire life, especially, by a commitment to study and a serious disciplined familiarity with modern culture" (*PDV* 72).

111 Cf. also *DMLP* 46.

112 James J. Gill, S.J., M.D., "The Study's Implications Related to Health," in Hoge, *The First Five Years of the Priesthood*, 122. Fr. Gill was the director of *The Christian Institute for the Study of Human Sexuality* in Chicago and the founder of the journal *Human Development*.

113 Cf. Congregation for Catholic Education, "Guide to the Training of Future Priests Concerning the Instruments of Social Communication," 19 March 1986, www.vatican.va/roman_curia/pontifical_councils/ pccs/_ documents/rc_pc_pccs_doc_19031986_guide-for-future-priests_en.html (downloaded 2/3/04), 19.

114 Ibid.

115 "The Media and the Family: A Risk and a Richness – Message of the Holy Father for the 38th World Day of Social Communications," 24 January 2004, www.vatican.va/news_services/bulletin/news/14258.   php?index=14258& po_date=24.01.2004&lang=en (downloaded 2/3/04), 1.

116 Ibid.

117 Cf. "Pornography and Violence in the Communications Media: A Pastoral Response," 7 May 1989, (www.vatican.va/roman_curia/pontifical_ councils/pccs/_documents/rc_pc_pccs_doc_07051989_pornography_ en.h ml [down-loaded 2/3/04], 29; cf. also two other documents from the same Pontifical Council issued together on 28 February 2002, "The Church and the Internet," 7 and "Ethics in Internet," 6). Pornography on the internet is a grave danger ll Christians, and in a particular way for the celibate priest. A few statistics will show the gravity of this addiction: "Sex is the No. 1 searched for topic on the Internet; 60% of all website visits are sexual in nature. There are 1.3 million pornographic websites — 20 times more than there were 5

years ago. More than 32 million unique individuals visited a porn site in Sept. of 2003. The total porn industry generates approximately $4 billion to $10 billion every year" ("Pornography's Internet Reach Undeniable," *National Catholic Register*, 17 December 2006).

118 R. Christian, "Priestly Spirituality," 56.

119 "Models for Ministry: Following the Vatican's Lead, the Church at all Levels is Addressing the Issue of Priestly Preparation and Continuing Formation," *Columbia*, June 2003, 23.

120 *The Battle for the American Church Revisited*, 142.

121 "The Continuing Formation of Priests," in *Priesthood: A Greater Love*, 280.

122 Congregation for the Clergy, "International Symposium: Concluding Message to all Priests of the World," 338. The bishops themselves have been held accountable to ongoing formation by Pope John Paul II: "For the Bishop, as for priests and religious, permanent formation is an intrinsic requirement of his vocation to mission" (*Pastores Gregis: On the Bishop, Servant of the Gospel of Jesus Christ for the Hope of the World* [Vatican City: Libreria Editrice Vaticana, 2003], 24).

123 O'Keefe, *In Persona Christi: Reflections on Priestly Identity and Holiness*, 27.

124 *ST* I, q. 36, a. 2.

125 "Priestly Spirituality," 56.

126 Aquinas wrote: "For even as it is better to enlighten than merely to shine, so is it better to give to others the fruits of one's contemplation than merely to contemplate" (*ST* II-II, q. 188, a. 6). This is also the "Dominican motto coined by St. Thomas Aquinas: 'To contemplate and give to others the fruits of contemplation' (*Contemplari et contemplata aliis tradere*)" (R. Christian, 53).

127 Timothy Costello, S.M., wrote: "A necessary condition for the formation of an authentic priestly identity is sufficient [and] accurate knowledge of the church's teaching especially about sacramental priesthood." This knowledge and formation must also be interiorized: "Internalized behaviour [...] is a unifying factor as attitudes and actions become personal convictions that are integral to the personality, manifestations of the actual and ideal self, and expressions of the person's deepest identity" (*Forming a Priestly Identity: Anthropology of Priestly Formation in the Documents of the VIII Synod of Bishops and the Apostolic Exhortation* Pastores Dabo Vobis [Roma: Editrice Pontificia Università Gregoriana, 2002], 237 and 214).

128 Marmion wrote to a confrère in April 1899 as he left Louvain,: "Fidelity to religious duties, Divine Office, mental prayer, spiritual reading,

is the source of the strength we need to carry out this will of God. That is why, although these practices are not the substance of sanctity, negligence in these duties leads inevitably to the more or less grave violation of the intrinsic obligations, and to the ruin of spiritual life" (*Union with God According to the Letters of Direction of Dom Marmion* [London: Sands & Co., 1934], 56-57).

Conclusion

The sacerdotal character is the foundation of the priestly life and its appropriation a source of renewal for the Church. Certainly one could elaborate on more ways the six themes presented above could be lived out, but a reflection on a few of the repercussions helps show the breadth of the issue. The proper understanding of the permanent nature of the priesthood is a stimulus for priestly fidelity, and as Fr. Aschenbrenner noted: "It will aid him in the joys and trials of priestly ministry."[1] Pope John Paul II reminded priests that the sacred character is a source of joy: "You are consecrated. Your whole being, down to its deepest fibre, is penetrated by the Holy Spirit who has conformed you to Christ to the glory of the Father. [...] Recognize and joyfully give witness to the fact of your consecration to God."[2]

This joy flows into gratitude for having been called, chosen, and loved by the Lord. Archbishop Buechlein wrote:

> Our very life exists *in persona Christi Capitis*. This awesome mystery can only move us priests to humble grateful prayer before the Tabernacle of him whose priesthood we serve. Daily we are moved to a double act of faith: (1) We believe that Christ calls us to this awesome ministry of his; and (2) since he does so, he gives us the grace we need to live this awesome call in humble service. Our challenge is to keep Christ as the center of our hearts and minds![3]

Awareness of God's love draws the priest to greater love and pastoral charity in his own life, a love he comes to know within himself and a love able to be manifested in his ministry. His priestly actions follow from the understanding of his priestly being.

Returning to the "two models" of the priesthood discussed in the second chapter, Msgr. Stephen Rossetti asks the question:

> Could we not have a priest who loves the sacraments and has a high theology of the priesthood, dressed in clerical garb and is faithful to the breviary, and at the same time, is pastorally sensitive, one who empowers the laity and is among them as servant? Are these two models mutually exclusive?"[4]

Rossetti says this can only happen when the clergyman is well balanced and properly formed, a man of communion. This is not merely the ideal but the goal. Proper knowledge and the integration of the sacramental character into the priestly life and ministry are fundamental for priests to be the men the Church needs them to be.

In *Ad Catholici Sacerdotii*, Pope Pius XI reflected on those attacking the Church of his own day. Almost seventy years later, his words hold even greater weight as the mass media explosion of this age continues to become more instantaneous and sensationalized, especially in the media frenzy of 2002. If the priesthood were not unique in its mission and professed dignity the world would not take notice, but that is not the case. Pope Pius XI encouraged the Church of his day not to lose heart; the same holds for the Church of today:

> A last tribute to the priesthood is given by the enemies of the Church. For, [...] they show that they fully appreciate the dignity and importance of the Catholic priesthood, by directing against it their first and fiercest blows; since they know well how close is the tie that binds the Church to her priests. The most rabid enemies of the Catholic priesthood are today the very enemies of God; a homage indeed to the priesthood, showing it the more worthy of honor and veneration.[5]

As the Church in America faces a weakening of morale amongst clergy and laity alike, this book is one of many contributions to the rebuilding of a stronger presbyterate and, consequently, a stronger people of God.[6] The Church must rebuild morale through doctrinal clarity and the promotion of moral virtue. The goal of this book is to hasten this renewal of the priesthood and the faith of all of the Baptized by returning to the sources of the Church's Traditional teaching of the priestly character.

On the occasion of the "World Day of Prayer for Vocations 2001," Pope John Paul II stated:

> The vocation to the ordained ministry *"is essentially a call to holiness in the form it derives from the sacrament of Holy Orders. Holiness is intimacy with God, it is the imitation of Christ, who was poor, chaste and humble; it is unreserved love for souls and a giving of oneself on their behalf and for their true good; it is a love for the Church which is holy and wants us to be holy, because this is the mission that Christ entrusted to her"* (*PDV* 33). Jesus calls the Apostles *"to be his companions"* (Mk. 3:14) in a privileged intimacy (cf. Lk. 8:1-2; 22:28). Not only does He share with them the mysteries of the Kingdom of Heaven (cf. Mt. 13:16-18), but He expects a surpassing faithfulness from them, constant with the Apostolic ministry to which He calls them (cf. Mt. 19:22-23), the humility of a servant who becomes the last of all (cf. Mt. 20:25-27). He asks of them faith in the powers they received (cf. Mt. 17:19-21), prayer and fasting as effective tools of the apostolate (cf. Mk. 9:29) and unselfishness: *"You have received without pay, give without pay"* (Mt. 10:8). From them He expects prudence together with simplicity and moral rectitude (cf. Mt. 10:26-28) and abandonment to Divine Providence (cf. Lk. 9:1-3; 19:22-23). They must be aware of the responsibilities

they assume, as they are administrators of the Sacraments established by the Master and laborers in His vineyard (cf. Lk. 12:43-48).[7]

This compendium of the priestly life lays out a plan of living a happy, healthy, and holy living. The first line of the quote above reminds the ordained that this call is "derived" from the Sacrament of Holy Orders. The sacerdotal gift and the life that flows from that gift deserve the response of holiness. God has given His priest the sacramental character as a gift for the good of the Church, and He gives them the strength to faithfully live their priesthood. Holiness is not an option for priests; the faithful have a right to be served by holy priests:

> The care of the spiritual life should be felt as a joyful duty on the part of the priest himself, and also as a right of the faithful who seek in him, consciously or not, the *man of God*, the counselor, the mediator of peace, the faithful and prudent friend, the sure guide to confide in during the more difficult moments in life to find encouragement and security (*DMLP* 39).

The New Evangelization needs new evangelists, priests unafraid to be who they are (cf. *PDV* 82).

Dogma and spirituality cannot be separated without harming the soul. Integration of "who one is" and "what one is supposed to do" by virtue of that calling is the task of the priest. The priestly vocation must be lived in love and holiness. Blessed Teresa of Calcutta encouraged priests to allow the love of Christ to shine forth from their lives:

> The priest today is the one who has been sent also, to be that living love, God's love for

the world today. The priest is that sign, he is the living flame, he is the sunshine of God's love for the world. So for the priest to be completely at the disposal of the Father he must be completely one with the Son, and utter and bring the love of the Father and the Son and the Spirit, in his life, in his attitudes, in his actions, because today God loves the world through each priest who takes the place of Christ himself. He is another Christ.[8]

This is the path of true joy and love for the priest. In closing, listen to the words of the man who continuously reminded priests to reclaim their priestly character, John Paul the Great:

> The call of the Lord Jesus still resounds today: "If anyone serves me, he must follow me" (Jn. 12:26). Do not be afraid to accept this call. You will surely encounter difficulties and sacrifices, but you will be happy to serve, you will be witnesses of that joy that the world cannot give. You will be living flames of an infinite and eternal love. You will know the spiritual riches of the priesthood, divine gift and mystery.[9]

The hope of the author of this book is that this study on the image and identity of the priesthood awaken a renewed interest among priests to foster intimacy with the Father, identification in the Son, and communion with the Holy Spirit. Thus, priestly holiness and fraternity can be renewed and the priestly character reclaimed in the Church of our day.

A Priest's Prayer of Consecration to Mary

O Holy and Immaculate Virgin Mary,
I consecrate to you the priesthood entrusted to me
by your Divine Son,
Jesus the Great High Priest.
I am all yours, and all that I have I give to you.
Be my tender and loving Mother, and remind me daily
that I am a beloved son of God the Father.
May your docile "yes" to the invitation of the Holy Spirit
inspire me to be a humble servant
of your Eucharistic Son
as He once again becomes incarnate in my hands.
Mary, you are the model of the Church, the Bride of Christ.
Help me to live a life worthy of my noble calling to be a
chaste spouse and spiritual father to the Church.
Reveal the beauty of your face
so that I may be comforted in my frustrations;
may I be purified and dwell within your Immaculate Heart
in union with the Sacred Heart of Jesus.
St. Joseph the Worker,
teach me to be the man the Father wants me to be:
laying down my life and sacrificing for my Bride
in the same way you cared for the Holy Family.
O Jesus, Divine Physician and Good Shepherd,
heal me that I might heal,
lead me that I might lead all people
into the Love of the Heart of the Trinity
where You live and reign
with the Father and the Holy Spirit,
One God forever and ever. Amen.

Notes

1 Aschenbrenner, *Quickening the Fire in Our Midst*, 81.

2 John Paul II, "Consecration to God and Service of Man Characterize Today's Apostle: Address to Priests, Religious, Seminarians and Novices in Padua," 12 September 1982, *ORE*, 4 October 1979, 6 and 7. "Our priestly life and activity continue the life and activity of Christ himself. Here lies our identity, our true dignity, the source of our joy, the very basis of our life" (*PDV* 18).

3 "The Sacramental Identity of the Ministerial Priesthood: *In Persona Christi*," in *Priests for a New Millennium: A Series of Essays on the Ministerial Priesthood by the Catholic Bishops of the United States*. ed. Secretariat for Priestly Life and Ministry (Washington, D.C.: USCC, 2000), 51. "The grateful heart, because it is selflessly oriented, always knows profound joy" (Aschenbrenner, *Quickening the Fire in Our Midst*, 106).

4 "The Priest as Man of Communion," in *Vocation Journal 2002* (Little River, South Carolina: National Conference of Diocesan Vocation Directors, 2002), 60.

5 Pius XI, *Ad Catholici Sacerdotii*, 30: *AAS* 28 (1936), 19.

6 There are several new books regarding priesthood and formation that have been published between 2004 and 2006 that are worth noting: Msgr. Charles Murphy, *Models of Priestly Formation: Past, Present, and Future*; Msgr. Stephen Rossetti, *The Joy of Priesthood*; Fr. Howard P. Bleichner, *View from the Altar: Reflections on the Rapidly Changing Catholic Priesthood*; Fr. Thomas Acklin, O.S.B., *The Unchanging Heart of the Priesthood*; Fr. Paul J. Philibert, O.P., *Stewards of God's Mysteries: Priestly Spirituality in a Changing Church*; Fr. Michael Heher, *The Lost Art of Walking on Water: Re-Imaging the Priesthood*, and Fr. Gerald Coleman, *Catholic Priesthood: Formation and Human Development*.

7 "Message of Pope John Paul II for the 39th World Day of Prayer for Vocations," *ORE*, 5 Dec. 2001, 3 (emphasis in the original).

8 Blessed Teresa of Calcutta, in *Testament, Constitutions, and Directory of the Missionaries of Charity Fathers*, 108.

9 John Paul II, "*The Son of Man Has Not Come to Be Served, But to Serve, and to Give His Life*: Message for the 40th World Day of Prayer for Vocations," *ORE*, 5 February 2003, 3.

Printed in the United States
218775BV00001B/7/P